TELOS AND TECHNOS

The Teleology of Economic
Activity and the Origins of Markets

Norman L. Roth

University Press of America,® Inc.
Lanham · Boulder · New York · Toronto · Plymouth, UK

Copyright © 2008 by
University Press of America,® Inc.
4501 Forbes Boulevard
Suite 200
Lanham, Maryland 20706
UPA Acquisitions Department (301) 459-3366

Estover Road
Plymouth PL6 7PY
United Kingdom

Library of Congress Control Number: 2007930452
ISBN-13: 978-0-7618-3847-0 (paperback : alk. paper)
ISBN-10: 0-7618-3847-3 (paperback : alk. paper)

Contents

Acknowledgments

I am especially grateful to my long suffering spouse Alice for putting up with me throughout this project and to Neil Murdock Cameron of Montreal Quebec and Leigh Urban Smith of Vancouver British Columbia, my own personal "wise guys" and anointed "enablers." Without them *Telos and Technos* would never have come to fruition. Many kudos are due my A-1 editor and layout designer, Dorothy Albritton of Majestic Wordsmith, whose patience and forbearance are truly formidable.

In the organic complex of habits and thought which make up the substance of an individual's conscious life, the economic interest does not lie isolated and distinct from all other interests.

—Thorstein Veblen

Economics is essentially a moral "science," and not a natural science. That is to say, it employs introspection and judgments of value.

—John Maynard Keynes,
letter to Roy Harrod in 1938

Consciousness cannot be computable.

—Roger Penrose

The conceptual anticipation of the future whose existence is a necessity in the nature of the present . . . This process is the teleological aim at some ideal in the future.

The event is the unit of all things real: every phenomenon may be analyzed into events.

—Alfred North Whitehead, 1938

It is the "end" that lends "means" its importance, not vice versa . . . There cannot be any doubt that there is a *causal* relationship between the importance of the end, and that of the means.

—Eugen Von Böhm-Bawerk

Chapter One

Introduction

The central problem of contemporary economic thought, especially the dominant neo-classical strain, would be resolved if the origins and causes of economic activity were reduced to their most elemental underlying motivations. In the context of this exposition, they are TECHNOS, the Promethean Imperative, the direct descendant of Thorstein Veblen's ancestral concept—the "Instinct of Workmanship"; and TELOS, the goals and "ends" of economic activity. Technos embodies the drive, the acquired skills and tools that enable mankind to work toward those ends, regardless of whether they are achieved in the form originally envisaged.

These basic behavioral drives are the closest and most irreducible that any man-made thing can get to the forces of nature. It will be demonstrated in subsequent chapters how Telos, especially its most important component, *the current conception of the standard of life* interacts with Technos in *the* crucial feedback relationship of economic life, to form the virtual state known as "the market"; and how the income levels which support the actual standard of living at a given point in economic history are the resultant state in a naturally lagged relationship, which is the primal characteristic of *the* crucial feedback between the two most basic economic motivations.

Further development of these basic ideas will demonstrate how the actual *quantity of work needed* (not congruent with employment) at a particular point along the trajectory of *technological time* (related to Henri Bergson's concept of durée) is itself a resultant state of the Telos-Technos feedback, which will be defined as the *Natural Participation Rate*. All this is tantamount to explaining why (Telos) and how (Technos) economic activity "happens" in the first place. The feedback relationships that characterize the interaction of Telos and Technos are causal ones that are inherently *non* tautological and *dependent* on the trajectory of past economic history and *cognitive* behavior. They are inevitably of a contingent nature. Indeed, to even attempt to describe the events caused by the Telos-Technos interaction as "deterministic" is to obscure rather than clarify them—which is usually the stated goal of those who grasp at the mirage of spurious "quantifiability" and exactitude, where only a general direction is discernable. Therefore, the roots of uncertainty in economic analysis lie in the Telos-Technos interactive process, which is itself value-loaded because of Telos; and inherently prone to *hystereses* at every level of economic behavior because economic behavior, like all human behavior, is rooted in basic anthropology and social psychology, which can only generate time-path dependent (not *dead clock* time), lagged responses. Hystereses is used here in its most basic and generic sense; that is, the lagging in observed response and effect of an entity when the forces acting on it are changed.

Thus the role of *timing* (the synchronization phenomenon) and *time* (path dependency) evolves naturally from an explanation of economic activity and *work* based on the non-tautological consequences of Telos interacting with Technos.

It will also be demonstrated in this exposition—which is *macro* oriented—that the relationship between macro-economic events and micro-economic ones is *gestalt* in nature and therefore not amenable to the spurious exactitude of continuous aggregation. *Gestalt*, will have its conventional meaning here—as in other social sciences—of an entity that behaves as something more than the simple sum of its parts; this is also a natural consequence, rooted in the Telos-Technos feedback relationship.

As this exposition develops, it will be demonstrated that the arguments presented owe a debt of gratitude to the insights of the great economic thinkers of the past, especially some of their more philosophic and intuitive probings. These will be quoted and connected in their historical context as they become relevant to the text. Thus the writer emphatically connects his material to the history of economic thought—on the same issues that were always there. We are all "time-path dependent."

The Domain of Say's "Law"; McCulloch's "Law" of Automatic Compensation

It should be stated at the outset that technology is endogenous to this model of economic activity. It is not simplistically regarded as a shock force that intrudes on the otherwise harmonious universe of steady-state equilibrium growth paths; Technos, the Promethean imperative, is embodied (endogenized) in this model as "technological time" and is accepted as an omnipresent force in human behavior that cannot by itself determine the trajectory of economic events. Technologies are *not*, therefore, a kind of *deus ex machina* generated spontaneously out of a nearly infinite set of potential combinations of already existing techniques, tools, skills, and technologies. They are created out of their interaction with Telos—especially the *current conception of the standard of life* component.

Since technology is treated as an endogenous variable (developed as the concept of technological time), a Telos-Technos model of economic activity lies outside the *legitimate* domain of Say's "law." In chapter four it will be explained that when technological time is constant—in effect the same thing as keeping technology out of the scope of economic enquiry by banishing it to the exogenous netherworld (outside the "field" both literally and metaphorically)—then it is impossible to disprove Say's "law" in its "strong" form, and its Walrasian/Marshallian extensions and ramifications.

It will also be demonstrated how—to paraphrase Georgescu-Roegen's comment about the production-spatial metaphor—McCulloch's "law" of automatic compensation is the "deepest, unobtrusive," and most insidiously hidden fallacy in macro-economic theory, and by neutralizing any non-deterministic explanation of the role of technology as being a natural one, it set the stage for more than a century of neo-classical exile into the exogenous netherworld. All this, despite the fact that classical economists discussed it, debated it, and recognized its primacy continuously and that an awareness of its role as a primal force in human behavior has stimulated imaginative comment since the ancient Greeks (the myth of Prometheus and the Titans, the archetype of the Demiurge, etc.) nearly three millennia ago.

The McCullochian fallacy has outcropped into economic literature in many guises, some of them in the form of moral posturing, some as Polyanna optimism, and also as naïve crankery . . . as in the "Technocracy" movement. But, as will be argued in later chapters, this deterministic superstition was the grandmother of many more, from Marx to the neo-classical physio-crats.

Of major importance in this exposition is the impact of the Telos-Technos relationship on the definition, valuation, role, and durability of capital, as well as its capacity to be usefully "measured"; and as will be demonstrated, the best of the capital theory of the past, (e.g., Joan Robinson, vintage models of Samuelson-Dorfman, bias theory, human capital concepts) were often legitimate and revealing attempts to reach beyond the contraints of the Neo-classical mindset. The conclusions of the sections on Capital and technological time lean heavily toward the "Capital is as Capital does" philosophy of Joan Robinson; and toward a more taxonomic approach to describing the role of capital functioning through technological time.

Chapter Two

Telos and the Current Conception of the Standard of Life

> As a matter of *selective* necessity, man is an agent. He is, in his own apprehension, a centre of *unfolding, impulsive* activity—"teleological" activity. He is an agent *seeking* in every act the accomplishment of some concrete, objective, impersonal *end*. . . .
>
> —Thorstein Veblen,
> *The Theory of the Leisure Class*, Chapter I

Teleological explanations of action have been largely extruded from the natural sciences, even if we take account of the doctrine of "vitalism" which proved to be the most stubborn and chameleon-like of adversaries. After all, it is no longer a subject of credible speculation to attribute goal-seeking or purpose to bodies (individual or collective) that are considered to lack consciousness.

However, such explanations of behavior and their resultant consequences *are* of crucial relevance in the behavioral sciences and in forming judgments in the daily business of life—where the values, preferences, motivational beliefs, and purposes of people and their institutions are of vital operational interest. To circumvent them—or to seek to "rise above" them (via exalted supra-deterministic forces) . . . or what is equivalent in practice, to treat them as just "being there" in the form of "given" items on a "menu" of commodities or "unexplained factor endowments" *without ontogeny*—is to create a self-neutering *cordon sanitaire* between the entire subject and the real world which *is* dependent on its historical trajectory.

These considerations alone should have (by the mid-20th Century at latest) made the physical sciences of the mid-19th Century a particularly inappropriate role model for emulation by the human sciences, especially *economics*, either openly or, especially, covertly and subliminally.

The ultimate motivational forces impelling all forms of economic activity arc human want and the goals associated with those wants. When the teleological drive toward such wants manifests itself in some form of observable economic behavior by human beings functioning both as individuals or, collectively, through their institutions, then the identifiable range of goals, goods, and services that motivated such behavior is defined as the *operational* Telos of that society. The most important, but by no means the only important, subset of this *operational* Telos (henceforth designated by the Greek letter Omega: ω) are those components associated with satisfying the more obvious hedonistic and physical needs of individuals and their most natural institutions, e.g., the family, the company, the industry, the government, and the military. The range of good and services comprising this subset of omega is called the Current Conception of the Standard of Life (which I shall refer to as "CCSL" for convenience of description).

It may be thought of as a certain widely diffused notion regarding which particular goods and services constitute a currently acceptable mode of living at a particular point in chronological time for a particular society . . . *and what motivates economic behavior in that direction.*

Thus the relationship of the CCSL (in particular) to the popular idea of the standard of living may be described as a kind of beckoning "ghost" of a future standard of living that is lying just ahead of the present one. It affects the various forms of economic behavior (consuming, investing, saving, working, leisure, willingness to incur debt, labor unions' and managements' preconceived standards of a "living wage," etc.) each in their own way and exercises a profound and decisive influence on economic decisions, regardless of whether or not the decision-makers are consciously aware of the ultimate teleological horizons that are driving their behavior (See Appendix 8).

There are many examples of how the CCSL affects daily economic decision-making in direct but unobtrusive ways:

1.   A trade union's negotiating and "hold-out" time strategies may be fueled by preconceived visions of what "standard of living" their members' wages should be able to support. Management's negotiating

position can often be heavily and *explicitly* influenced by their preconceived "vision" of what the *differences* between the living standards of executive and line staff "ought" to be (See Appendix 8).

2. An investor's (individual or institutional) decision about where and in what firm his expectations for high returns are most probable is heavily influenced by whether it seems that the products and services those firms are producing will be accepted into the lifestyles of their "targeted" consumer markets in the future.

3. An individual's willingness to support installment debt is heavily influenced by the chosen product's "status-conferring image." This "image" is the "statement" it is making to his peers when its presence, in a soon-to-be-enjoyed standard of living, is noticed by them. (This is in agreement with Keynes' vision of consumers' behavior—*not* with the notion that consumers' spending is largely constrained by *real* income.)

4. The decisions of millions of families to have female spouses participate in the labor market. Such a decision is not only heavily value-loaded about the "role of women" in the labor force; it also is decisively driven by the "vision" of a higher standard of living that can be supported by the combined incomes of both partners and a *particular image* (see Appendix 9) of the array of goods and services (kind, quality, and quantity) that might not otherwise be affordable. Precautionary instincts to ensure that the envisioned lifestyle can be permanently sustained if one partner has to leave the labor market temporarily also play a major role. In the popular catch phrases of an earlier era, such aspirations were summed up as "a chicken in every pot," "a car in every garage," "every man can live like a king, every woman a queen," These are still not forgotten slogans.

5. Decisions to save may also be fueled by a kind of default behavior, as well as the traditional Keynesian motivations. For example, the amount saved may also be decisively affected by a consumer's cumulative *non*-purchasing of products and services that are no longer considered necessary for a previously envisioned CCSL. If there are a large number of such "default" savers, their "aggregate" impact will obviously affect the incomes and resultant living standards of other consumers. These are economic events that take place along the trajectory of economic history and along the life cycles of people and of the very commodities and services that constitute their CCSLs. They cannot be understood in the context of "givens" or "path independence."

These examples of the basic underlying power of an operational Telos to influence observable economic behavior are only the "tip of the iceberg." The reader can easily, even at this initial stage of the exposition, anticipate many more. The best way of generating realistic and operational cases is to begin with a tentative classification of elements comprising the CCSL, the most important sector of the operational Telos. The other, non-CCSL sector of Telos will be left to the end of the next section. But it is the balance between these two sectors which is determined by the collective, value-loaded will of society, changing and contending through time, that determines the nature of that society; and the kinds of conflicts that it enters into with other societies; *and the dominant institutions of that society.*

A Tentative Classification of Component Elements in the Current Conception of the Standard of Life

Category 1

This category consists of those elements that are considered indispensable to some irreducible and basic standard of comfort and security. Most of these elements are in the food, clothing, and shelter groups, and are considered "necessities of life." Others, such as automobiles, a wide array of electrical appliances and electronic products and services, and health and medical care above some widely accepted "bottom line" (regardless of how they are financed) are also deemed "mandatory" in most developed societies. Most of this category approximates the observable "standard of living" (see Appendix 9) in some periodically recorded, per capita "measurable" description and influences the "poverty line" standards—underlying the decisions and policies of those public officials concerned with various pension, unemployment, social welfare, and income supplement programs. The key point is to understand that the existing, perceived *standard of living*, however strongly it may be affecting all aspects of economic behavior (consumers, welfare officials, investors, labor organizations, etc.) is not the only category of the CCSL motivating observable economic behavior. This differentiation alone should, in itself, prevent the fallacy of congruency of the CCSL and the popular concept of the *standard of living*. Indeed, the existing, observed standard of living may not necessarily be the resultant state, i.e., what actually gets to be produced and consumed further along the trajectory of economic history. That depends on how *all* the elements of the CCSL and Telos interact with Technos and with each other. There is no intrinsic tendency to congruency; therefore, the process itself cannot be described as tautological.

Category 2

This category consists of those goods and services that are on the *positive* periphery of the first category. Such goods and services are in a state of transition with respect to incorporation into the more visible and "measurable" status of the *standard of living*. That is, they are on a sort of "threshold of consumption" with respect to acceptance or non-acceptance as a regular, enduring element in the standard of living. In terms of their present participation in the standard of living, they overlap with Category 1. The elements of this category consist not only of new additions in the kinds of goods and services, but changes in the quantity and quality of established ones. But the elements in this category are part of the CCSL because they are motivating various forms of observable economic behavior. In this case, "autonomous investment" is the type that is not "induced" by changes in the output or a previous period, but results from changes in the introduction of new goods and services and improvements in the range and quality of the old ones, and by activity in the various businesses associated with the advertising, promotional, and consumer information sector of the labor force. But none of the behavior caused by this category of the CCSL is of the nature of "automatic compensation." We will return to this topic in the last part of Chapter Four, dealing with the relationship of Telos and the CCSL to earlier ruminations on the same phenomena—in this case (obviously) those of Sir Roy Harrod. Hopefully it will clarify what Sir Roy was *quite legitimately groping for* and by putting it in the light of the Telos-Technos nexus, explain why it became so needlessly controversial.

Category 3

The third category of elements in the current conception of the standard of life consists of those elements that are on its negative periphery. That is, they are passing out of the scale of customary expenditure as observed by some estimate of declining per capita consumption of the relevant products and services and are therefore affecting current economic behavior accordingly.

At present (the 1990s) these elements might include cigarettes, various health care products judged ineffective or harmful, and certain modes of transportation. In the early years of the twentieth century they would have included whale-bone corsets, buggy whips, and the widespread use of horses for private and commercial transportation. The important thing to note is that these elements are at a late stage in their "life cycles" because of major shifts in tastes, lifestyles, cultural preferences, and the like. "Fad"-engendered products and services are very obviously part of this category, notoriously so in major sectors of the economy such as the garment industry, entertainment, and electronic goods and services. Conceivably, certain types of commercial real estate, such as concentrations of office towers (and even the built form itself) could suffer the fate of what machine guns did to massed cavalry charges—at the hands of portable "cyberspace"/computer products. This would certainly have a drastic effect on investment behavior, work choices, and associated manufacturing decisions—a classic example of the annihilation of capital value (or hyper-acceleration in the vintage of capital goods) caused by the action of an "ideal technology" functioning through technological time (to be defined in greater detail in later chapters).

One class of commodities in particular—antiques (or collectibles)—may be seen as an "overlap" between Categories 2 and 3. After having gone through its functional life cycle in the CCSL, it passes out of Category 3, only to reappear on the positive periphery years later as a recrudescence in value of the surviving specimens. This is an authentic re-emergence into the domain of "Giffen commodities" by way of scarcity value, and the teleology of buyers. It's a clear example of the cognitive trajectory of past economic events affecting current, observable, economic behavior, without resorting to "given" menus of commodity choices. This latter, utility-oriented concept is incompatible with a model of economic activity that emphasizes time-path dependency (see Appendix 1).

Sector 2 of Omega (ω)

The non-CCSL sector of Telos consists of those goods and services that do not arise from the hedonistically-oriented economic behavior of individuals manifesting itself in "natural" marketplaces. Indeed, an important consideration about such elements of the operational Teloses of society is that they cannot be activated without the intervention of willful institutional behavior, which is either imposed from above, or collectively assented to by all of—or a significant part of—the population. (Note Hayek's idea of an economy based on a uniform will. See Joseph Salerno on Wieser's and Hayek's uncomfortable consideration of General Equilibrium.) This sector may be further subdivided into the various levels of government or the many non-governmental institutions that constitute "civil society." The term "public sector" is sometimes used to denote the activity of the various levels of government. On other occasions the term is understood, rather ambiguously, to include educational institutions, financial institutions, research organizations, and the armed forces.

In any case, these elements of Telos and the products, services, and types of work associated with them cannot be activated without some form of periodic collection of funds—taxes, voluntary donations, premiums, user fees, tithes, surcharges, and the like. They employ many of the same factors of production (capital ensembles, skills, and motivations) that would be used to supply the elements of the CCSL. Moreover, throughout history societies have been labeled and stereotyped according to how they chose to divide their resources among such teleologies, and how much economic activity they chose to divert from the CCSL. It often determined the frequency and nature of their conflicts with other societies. Such non-CCSL operational Teloses were, of course, far more ideologically and anthropologically value-loaded than their counterparts in the CCSL.

In effect, throughout recorded history (including our own times) a significant amount of economic activity has been fueled by *non*-economic (i.e., non-CCSL) goals.

Insofar as the economy's available factors of production are concerned, it matters little whether or not the products and services they produce are directed toward the more hedonistic goals embodied by the CCSL, or consumed by the great institutions of society for political, strategic, ideological, social, or military ends. Either way such output can be quantified and delivered to whoever demanded it, for goals such as hydro-electric dams, freeways, municipal recreation facilities, or Olympic swimming pools, for instance. Other goals could be in the category of ballistic missiles, space programs, aircraft carrier task forces, or hospitals. In earlier times, these would have included pyramids, temples, aqueducts, cathedrals, art (regardless of taste and intended usage), social welfare programs, educational institutions, and great armies. All such operational teleologies are heavily value-loaded and arrived at through painful or inspired turmoil, conflict between the different classes and institutions of society and conflict with other societies who may feel threatened by the operational Teloses of their neighbors. All of them affect the observable economic behavior of investors (both government and private), taxpayers, consumers, and businesses who supply them, thereby diverting their productive resources from those goods and services normally associated with the CCSL.

The Cult of "Shocks" as "Proxies" for the "Exogeneous" in the Neo-Classical Paradigm

If almost anything—by way of the consequences of human action (individually and collectively)—that cannot be explained by the equilibrium/field metaphor, is described as a "shock," then nothing is a shock. (To paraphrase Frederick the Great, "A commander in the field who tries to defend everything ends by defending nothing.") Or, the door is wide open for the very "nihilism" that the aficionados of the neo-classical orthodoxy habitually attribute to George Shackle, Ludwig Lachmann and many "Austrian" school economists.

The wider the boundaries of the "land of the exogenous," the greater the hunger becomes for some kind of "lawful regularity" (or even forced symmetry), in order to combat "the dark forces of time and ignorance" (Keynes). It is worth noting that the knee-jerk resort to "explanation by shock" has now been elevated to a new field of "study." Real business cycle theory believes that shocks cause "unnatural" deviation from the "steady-state equilibrium growth paths" that are built-in "up front" into the neo-classical fantasy. This fantasy is that economic history can be—indeed, ought to be—"predictable" as an intrinsically positive series of events (with growth congruent with "development"). These events are easily represented by time-series analysis . . . with an underlying revelation of a one-to-one correspondence between chronological time and "progress." At least there finally seems to be a kind of "sotto voce" acknowledgement that the observations of "shocking" economic events are more "real" than the construct that they are "deviating" from.

In the static world of the equilibrium-field metaphor, alternate "t" paths arise naturally out of different assumptions about the responses of "agents" to various "shocks," stimuli, "externalities," "surprises," etc., within the same Walrasian boundary conditions. Consequently, an almost uncountable set of "t" series can be generated from whatever combination of stimuli and "shocks" are "applied" to whatever frame of mind such agents are in.

At the same time, new technologies and improvements to older ones are being continuously formed as the consequences of whatever detailed goals are generated by the operational Teloses of society at the time. For example, in ancient Egypt the ideological values that gave rise to pyramid building also caused major innovations in surveying, masonry, haulage of heavy materials, and the like. The teleology of imperial Rome resulted in the first great building of utilities and infrastructure in the Western and Mediterranean worlds, i.e., the imperial system of roads, linking the main centers of the empire to ensure maximum speed of travel for the legions; and the brilliantly engineered aqueducts, built by the imperial government with the labor and taxes of their subjects which, in turn, contributed to an increase in the scale of urban life in the ancient world, and the larger number of populous cities that developed. It is left to the reader to think of many more examples of this process, both ancient and modern. There is rich and abundant literature to be exploited for such illustration, but this literature does not "fit" comfortably with the pseudo-scientific posturing of static equilibrium models and "field" theories of economic choice. These theories purport to be independent (in production *and* consumption) of the trajectory of economic and technological history, with virtually all the key variables of economic thought simply "given," or "being there." The resultant human behavior is depended upon to be "automatic"—perfectly synchronized, and bedeviled only by various "rigidities" and intrusive shocks from exogenous interlopers, such as technological change and major shifts in operational teleologies.

In an explanation of the existence of economic activity based on a Telos-Technos nexus, it *is* what *was* previously considered "given" and exogenous "shocks" that are the key operational *variables* of economics. "Rigidities" are often the natural consequences of the Telos-Technos interaction, not intrusions or monkey wrenches thrown into the "mechanisms" of otherwise automatic, smoothly clearing market systems.

For example, if no demands for increased wage and salary benefits were fuelled by changes in the CCSL and perfectly natural public perceptions of the potential of technological capabilities, this kind of "rigidity" (essentially a state of non-responsiveness to observations of the economic environment) should constitute a veritable business utopia—until the inevitable fall in demand relative to increased productive capacity.

What is, of course, the source of ritualized conflict between labor and capital is in reality a lack of *rigidity*, i.e., the tendency of wage demands to insist upon an upward trend, perceived by employers to be an almost irreversible inertia that does not respond to the competitive cost rigours of the (virtual) market. But the awareness of new horizons of consumption opportunities, expanded by continuously improving technological capabilities, constitutes a set of variables that do not motivate employers in the same way that they motivate labor. Thus, that which stimulates employers' investment expectations is also confounding adjustments in their cost curves, through its quite different effect on the economic behavior of labor.

The Current Conception of the Standard of Life as Non-Automatic, Cognitive/Path-Dependent Behavior

If the CCSL did not exist as a motivator of change in economic behavior, then virtually all investment behavior would be of the "induced" variety, i.e., directly related to the growth of output/income of an historically similar period (within the same "technological time").

For our purposes this is represented by Hick's "elementary" case:

$$I_i = v \left\{ Y_{(t-1)} - Y_{(t-2)} \right\} \ldots\ldots\ldots\ldots\ldots\ldots\ldots\ldots\ldots\ldots\ldots\ldots\ldots (1)$$

Where I_i =   Investment (an increment to the stock of capital)
         v =   a percentage less than 1, itself dependent on the capital output ratio through *technological* time* and impacting on the accelerator., i.e., $v = f(\Upsilon)$
         Y =   Income received from the production of output
         t-1 =   represents the *chronological time* (i.e., durations) immediately preceding the present one (t), (t-2) the one immediately preceding (t-1) . . . etc. and Υ is technological time.

*e.g., If the capital output ratio is declining through *technological* time, a given increase in real output will be associated with a declining increment of capital "stock" for its support.

Further, in an attempt to put these concepts into Keynesian terms,

$$A_t = A \, (CCSL_{cat.2}; \, \mho) \quad \text{...} \quad (2)$$

Where $A_t =$ autonomous investment at time "t"
$CCSL_{(cat.2)}$ represents the current conception of the standard of life, specifically those elements of Category 2.
    $\mho$ represents *technological* time.

The preceding relationships in (2) are in accordance with conventional definitions of autonomous investment, which is motivated by changes in the technology of production and in the range of available products and services on the consumption horizon.

Also, $C_t = f \, (CCSL, Y_{t-1}) \quad \text{...} \quad (3)$

where $C_t =$ consumption at time t

and

if economic activity arising from sector 2 of ω (omega) is *not* included in autonomous investment, then:

$$I_{g\&cs} = f(\omega_{[sect.2]}, \, \mho) \quad \text{...} \quad (4)$$

Where $I_{g\&cs}$ represents investment by government and civil society
    $\omega_{[sect.2]}$ is the operational Telos of government and civil society

and

$$y_t = f(CCSL_{cat.1} \, ; \, Y_{t-1, \, t-2. \, \ldots .t-n}) \quad \text{..} \quad (5)$$

where y_t is income injected into the stream of Gross National income at time t (and spent during time t), by government and civil society in the form of income supplement programs, pension income, social welfare payments, and the like, which are in turn extracted from the Gross National incomes (Y) of previous time (fiscal) periods, t-1, t-2 . . . . . t-n (refer to "Classification of Component Elements," Category 1 earlier in this chapter).

Thus, received Gross National income at time t is given by the sum of relationships, (1) + (2) + (3) + (4) + (5). That is,

$$I_i + A_t + C_t + I_{g\&cs} + y_t = Y$$

or, regrouped.

$$Y = (C_t + y_t) + (I_i + A_t + I_{g\&cs}) \dots\dots\dots\dots\dots\dots\dots\dots\dots (6)$$

There is no intention in the statements of relationships (1) to (5) to suggest that variables like CCSL and omega are in any way capable of being defined and "measured" as homogeneous, aggregatable variables that may be manipulated to some sort of advantage not inherent in the concepts themselves, or not critically accounted for.

As will be demonstrated in Chapter Three (Technological Time) and Chapter Five (Capital), even traditional variables like "capital" or "investment" cannot be depended upon to behave like homogeneous, measurable, integrable variables when attempts are made to compare and analyze them from one successive technological time to the next. The preceding material is intended as a convenience to most readers who are accustomed to the notation and symbols of Keynesian analysis, in the hope that it will differentiate the conceptual framework of the Telos-Technos nexus. I leave it to the reader to judge whether or not the two systems are capable of achieving a "good fit." The same should have been admitted about such entities as Utility and Production functions long ago.

The Consumption Accumulation Process as a Contingent, Inherently Non-Automatic Process

Consumers are not "knee-jerk" robots that increase their wants and effective demand automatically, in perfectly synchronized response to those improvements in the technology of industry, which increase the capacity to "satisfy" them. Instead, consumer behavior should be thought of as a lagged response to received stimuli from the economy in the form of real price change, accumulated product knowledge, and perceptions about the state of contemporary technology. Indeed, consumers can be envisaged as being in a condition of temporary indecision, *between* a state of frenzied, "joyless" insatiability (see Appendix 2) *and* a Savonarola-like, holy frugality, rejecting all pleadings from Categories 1 and 2 of the CCSL to put out more hedonism.

In effect, consumers respond to their understanding of what is being offered in the marketplace by cognitive behavior operating through the economic institutions that support them, however imperfectly.

The Threshold of Conception—An Alternative Model of Consumers' Behavior in Increasing Consumption Beyond the Established Elements in the Present "Standard of Living"

Any general increases in the average *real* incomes of consumers that arise from advances in technological time (not the only source of such increase) will signal themselves over time to the consumption sector of the economy, and can occur in any one of a number of ways and combinations thereof:

Let *a* be an element of the *existing standard of living*

Denote *Money* income (wages, salaries, investment income, dividends, etc.) by *W*.

Suppose we consider an existing standard of living with an *array* of just one element—*a*.

Then, a rise in real income originating from improvements in the technology of producing and distributing *a* might signal itself to consumers in any of the following ways:

1. *W* increases, but the price of *a* remains constant.
2. Both *W* and the price of *a* increase, but *W* increases relatively more.
3. Price of *a* falls, but *W* remains constant (a typical scenario in the life cycles of electronic and electric products, services, and appliances since the early years of the twentieth century).
4. *W* increases and *a* decreases (above comments also appropriate).
5. *W* decreases, but the price of *a* decreases relatively more.

This makes a total of five ways that a rise in real income can signal itself to the consumer.

Now, consider a standard of living with two elements, *a* and *b*. A rise in *real* income might signal itself to consumers in any one of the following ways:

1. *W* remains constant, but the prices of *a* and *b* decrease.
2. *W* remains constant but the price of *a* decreases while the price of *b* either remains constant or increases relatively less (two ways).
3. *W* remains constant, while the price of *b* decreases, while the price of *a* either remains constant or increases relatively less (two ways).
4. *W* increases but *a* and *b* remain constant.
    i. *W* increases but *a* remains constant and *b* either decreases or increases relatively less.
    ii. The same as (i) except *b* remains constant and *a* is active in the same way as *b* in (i).
    iii. *W* increases while *a* and *b* decrease.
5.
    i. *W* decreases while *a* and *b* both decrease more.
    ii. *W* decreases, *a* remains constant, and *b* decreases relatively more.
    iii. Same as (ii) but *a* and *b* reversed.
    iv. Same as (ii) and (iii) except that instead of *a* or *b* remaining constant, the net sum of an increase in *a* and a decrease in *b* amounts to a greater (net) decrease than *W* (relatively).

i.e.,

Time	$\underline{W}$	Price of *a*	Price of *b*
t	100	10	10
t+1	95	12	2

i.e.,   At time *t* a lower percentage of money income is being spent on $(a+b)$. Therefore, for two elements in the standard of living there are a total of 16 ways in which an increase in real income may be signaled to consumers.

Consider a standard of living with three elements, *a*, *b*, and *c* and money income *W*.

Then in this case a rise in real income will occur if:

1. W remains constant but a, b, and c all fall.
2. W remains constant but *either a, b,* or c fall = 3 ways.
3. W remains constant while any two elements taken two at a time decrease in price while the third remains constant = $_3C_2$ = 3 ways.
4. W remains constant, any one of the elements increases in price while the other two each decrease more than one has increased = 3 ways.
5. W remains constant, any two of the elements increase in price, while the third decreases more than the other two = $_3C_2$ ways = 3 ways.
6. W increases, a, b, and c remain constant.
7. W increases, any one element remains constant while the other two decrease = 3 ways.
8. W increases, any one element decreases while the other two remain constant = 3 ways.
9. W increases, a, b, and c all increase relatively less, or all decrease = 2 ways.
10. W increases, any one element increases relatively less while the other two remain constant = 3 ways.
11. W increases, any elements taken two at a time increase less, while the third either remains constant or decreases = $2 \cdot {}_3C_2$ = 6 ways.
12. W increases, one element remains constant, one element increases relatively less, one element decreases = $2 \cdot {}_3C_2$ = 6 ways.
13. W increases, a, b, and c all decrease more.
14. W decreases, any two elements decrease relatively more while the third either remains constant or increases relatively less = $2 \cdot {}_3C_2$ = 6 ways.
15. W decreases, any one element decreases relatively more while the other two either remain constant or increase relatively less, = 3 x 2 = 6 ways.
16. W decreases, one element decreases much more, one remains constant and the other increases relatively less than the other decreases = 6 ways.

This makes a total of 56 ways in which real income increases may occur for a standard of living consisting of three elements.

For a standard of living with four elements the number of ways in which a rise in real income can occur is about 216.

I will not belabor the reader's patience (or my own) any further.

If this growing recombinant functional relationship is pursued further, it will prove to be, in general, more powerful than exponential growth in generating the number of ways in which an increase in productivity of the various elements in the existing standard of living may be signaled to the consumer. It is not being suggested that improvements in productivity are the only source of real price decrease in an open economy; or that real price increases arising from other non-technical sources (exchange rates, value-added taxes, monetary inflation) cannot dampen their real income or substitution effects.

In effect, any rise in real income is a signal transmitted to the consumer that the productive capacity of the economy—in terms relevant to the elements of the standard of living *that (s)he knows*—has improved; and that the consumer has reached a new frontier of consumption opportunity, wherein (s)he may decide to add *newly perceived* products and services to the established ones in the current standard of living, or buy already established ones on a more generous scale, both quantitatively and qualitatively.

It is evident that even the transmission of a rise in real income (only the first step of the consumption accumulation process—the "trigger" so to speak) is itself the net result of a stochastic/contingent, and time-consuming passage through the various institutions of the economy (from lab or factory to the consumer's consciousness). This process cannot be anything other than the very antithesis of McCulloch's "Theory of Automatic Compensation" . . . even in its "weak" form, which allows for a slow period of adjustment that may result in "pockets" of unemployed factors of production, but not the possibility of long-term, structural unemployment (or "glut," in the language of classical economists).

It is, of course, not surprising why the Theory of Automatic Compensation, in its most subliminal form, is so favored by devotees of static equilibrium analysis and "field" theories of consumers' and producers' behavior. After all, it enables them to ignore the "discontinuities" which the far richer body of empirical knowledge (that comes with an acceptance of the trajectory of economic and technological history) reveals to be the core of our understanding. It is much easier to banish the ontogeny of economic phenomena into the exogenous netherworld in favor of describing the virtual, unexplained fantasy world of "field" (utility and technology) and "shocks" to "steady state equilibrium growth paths" by predatory intruders such as technological change.

As has been described, the number of ways in which signals of real income growth can occur depends on the number of elements in Category 1 and 2 of the CCSL, during the last (marginal) time period, prior to changing of the consumer's consumption behavior on the *threshold* of the CCSL. In effect, the *frequency* with which established patterns of consumption are being "disturbed" by the more or less continuous "pressure" of such "signals" is also increasing as the number of elements in the first category of the CCSL increases arithmetically.

Of course, the individual probabilities that any one of these possible ways (that an increase in real income may be signaled) would occur at a given time are not equal; there is undoubtedly a typical probability distribution during a particular *era* of technological time. Also, each way in which such signals can be triggered has a realistic range of value "weights" it can take at a specific time, which also has a specific probability distribution of its own. The resultant effect of these underlying considerations may well be that the probability (that the increase in real income expected lies within a fairly limited range of values) may be quite high.

Whatever their net result (in terms of real income change), none of these events will manifest themselves in meaningful economic behavior from the consumer until that point at which their cumulative impact attains some sort of *critical increment* at the decision threshold of Category 2 of the CCSL.

Any increase in real income of consumers (or in the *average* real income) will not necessarily trigger automatically a corresponding increase in Category 2 of the CCSL—and hence in the level of economic activity associated with such changes in consumption behavior.

Therefore let the real income "frontier" at which a decision regarding an increase in Category 2 of the CCSL is being made be denoted by Y_{Υ} where Υ stands for technological time.

Let that rise in real income beyond Y_{Υ}, necessary to just induce her to add a unit of commodity (or service x) at *real* price $P_x\delta$ of $CCSL_{[cat.2]}$ be denoted as ΔY_{δ}.

Therefore the Threshold of Consumption at Υ is given by

$$\theta = \frac{\Delta Y_{\Upsilon}}{P_x\delta}$$

where: ΔY_{Υ} is the Critical Increment expressed as the required increase of real income, in indexed form, over and above $Y_{\Upsilon} = 100$ (see Appendix 4).

   P_x is the real price of a consumable unit of commodity x expressed as p / W_{Υ} where p is the money price of a unit of x at T and real income frontier Y_{Υ} and W_{Υ} is money income at Y_{Υ}.

Then, the real price of x is expressed as a percentage weight (x 100) of money income W_{Υ} at income (real) frontier Y_{Υ}.

$$\theta = \frac{\Delta Y_{\Upsilon}}{P_{x100} / W_{\Upsilon}} = \frac{(\Delta\, Y_{\Upsilon}\, W_{\Upsilon} \div 100)}{p}$$

Therefore, in this model of consumption accumulation, the consumer is always considered to be at a given "frontier" of real income at a specific point in the trajectory of technological time and confronted with a specific price of commodity x of Category 2 of the current conception of the standard of life. Indeed, this simple model of consumer motivation demonstrates just how subjective the notion of "affordability" really is. The most important word in the definition of the "Critical Increment" is "induce." A high critical increment will be generated by a high threshold of consumption, given the price of commodity x confronting the consumer at the real income frontier. But what lies behind that critical increment?

Those institutions of the economy which are variously described as the advertising industry, promotional functions, public relations, motivational research, marketing research, industrial propaganda, etc. and their complementary institutions—the financial institutions concerned with the extension of commercial and consumers' credit—which give rise to the phenomenon of installment buying and chattel lending.

These perfectly normal functions and associated institutions and occupations, which have given rise to no end of moral posturing, and ritualistic vituperation, are seen to be both indispensable and natural in an economy described by the interaction of Technos and the CCSL—and toward braking precipitous declines in the *Natural Participation Rate* (see Chapter Four). Therefore, a highly developed performance standard by the advertising and marketing institutions of the economy are needed to overcome any Savonarola-like, holy frugality that may hinder the contribution of Category 2 of the CCSL toward absorbing the benefits of increases in the productive capacity of industry. Indeed, if there were any substance at all to the "law" of automatic compensation, the advertising, promotional and consumer-motivational industries could not possibly exist on the scale that they have for most of the 20th century. But the neo-classical fantasy world of "givens" in ontogeny-shy "fields" and static production functions, makes it virtually impossible to explain how these perfectly valid economic functions ever appeared on the trajectory of economic history in the first place.

Rather than devise artificial examples of the applicability of the previous material (in graphic or tabular form), it would be far more illuminating to design empirical surveys and tests based on the rich body of market research techniques and data (archival and contemporary) that have been available for most of the century in many countries. For example, the product categories and services to be examined could include such examples as:

1. Ownership of second motor vehicles, historical trends, associated changes in real income and real prices of products co-related with socio-economic class of consumers.

2. Empirical testing of Engel's "law": As real income levels increase, the percentage of income spent on food consumption declines. This principle is considered to apply most strongly to unembellished food staples. What does Engel's law really look like if it is analyzed on a multi-variate basis? This would take into account data from different cultures, socio-economic classes, changes in the productive technology of food, tastes in products and perceived health considerations, the growth in range of products appearing in Category 2 of the CCSL, and the life cycles (i.e., ontogenies) of different products on the historical trajectory of the CCSL.

3. Different tastes for the wide range of electronic and cybernetic products offered, by age groups and different national cultures. For example, at the present time (1990s) the appetite for personal computers and video games by *domestic* consumers (non-industrial usage) appears to be much stronger in the Far East than in some European countries, (e.g., France, Italy, U.K.) while the appetite for reading books (affecting both the retail publishing industry and public library institutions) is still quite robust in Western Europe. This is often referred to colloquially as being a "toy market." (Is the taste for many such products likely to develop into an "anabasis" from $CCSL_{[cat. 2]}$ to $CCSL_{[cat. 3]}$?)

4. The economic history of demand for large appliances (refrigerators, freezers, washing machines, dryers, radios, au-

dio systems, television, etc.). This would amount to a "life cycle" (evolutionary) study of the incorporation of such products into the CCSL from the peripheral Category 2 into Category 1 and in some cases a discharge into Category 3. (e.g., an attempt in the 1950s to mass market an appliance called the *Gladiron*: a large roller-hot iron for pressing bed clothes, shirts, dresses, etc. that required the domestic user to operate the appliance in her own home much the same way as a commercial laundry. A suitably contoured operator's seat came with the Gladiron. It enjoyed approximately a three-year life cycle in the marketplace.

More typically the history of annual domestic demand for refrigerator units in the United States from 1937 to 1963 was:

Year	Number of Units Sold (millions)
1937	2.5
1941	3.5
1950	5.0
1958	3.0
1963	3.0

Despite the distorting influence of World War II and the release of "pent-up" demand culminating in the Korean War "buying panic" of 1950, the pattern of demand through time is obvious. By 1958 refrigerators were firmly and predictably established in the standard of living, more or less equivalent to Category 1 of the CCSL. They had completely penetrated the market (95% of all households). As such, a "saturation" point was achieved, wherein demand became increasingly predictable as a simple function of replacement demand and household formation.

The only variations from established patterns of predictability were themselves predictable, i.e., if and when the threshold of consumption for more than one unit per household (associated with Category 2 of the CCSL) declined, this underlying change in consumer motivation would be reflected in time-lagged shifts to the right of associated demand curves and in changes to their curvature (see Appendix 3).

In the relationship $\theta_x\delta = \dfrac{\Delta Y_\delta}{P_x\delta}$

it would be interesting to explore the interpretations *in terms of economic behavior* of sequentially varying the terms in the expression that defines the Threshold of Consumption at Y_δ and n = number of elements in Category 2 of the CCSL.

For example, what is the economic behavior and the motivations behind it if the real price P of commodity x was cut in half but the critical increment remained constant? Arithmetically, the Threshold of Consumption would be doubled. Whatever the identity of product x of Category 2 of the CCSL (either a newly perceived one or some qualitative or quantitative extension of one already present in $CCSL_{[cat.\ 1]}$), this scenario implies that there is something about x or any extension thereof, that made it an even higher barrier to consumption *after* (see Appendix 4) achieving an increase in real income that *in the recent past* would have triggered a purchase of x at twice its current price. The most obvious interpretation is to invoke "Giffen's paradox" as a consequence of the other income effects that produced ΔY_δ in the first place (see Appendix 5), plus the incremental income effect of reducing the price of commodity x, combined with the substitution effect of other elements of the CCSL, which may now tempt the consumer as a consequence of her higher income status. In effect, a significant change in observable economic behavior has taken place, directly attributable to "signals" of real income improvements caused by technical change, interacting with the CCSL. In a Telos-Technos nexus, Giffen's "paradox" may not be all that "paradoxical," nor is it an automatic, easily predictable event. It has simply become a "possible" event with some assignable probability in the contingent universe of economic events. Arguably, the combination of the flow of technological time, as a permanent source of change in real income, *with* the constant fluctuations in the elements of the CCSL, generates continuous increases in the complexity of modern economies; and this phenomenon, more than any other consideration, is the "tap root" of the uncertainty that is so much more obvious than any artificial construct, such as stable equilibrium growth paths or automatic, "self-correcting," market clearing "mechanisms."

The reader should explore the economic interpretations of all possible combinations of the variables. It would be illuminating to incorporate actual examples from the history of consumers' behavior in such "thought experiments."

In summation, the process by which additional elements are incorporated into the CCSL is essentially a *discrete and contingent* one wherein consumers respond to "signals" which are transmitted as subjectively received real price changes, in an appropriate *time* frame. Since these "signals" have to travel through the media of human behavior and the institutional structure of the economy, and the "signals" themselves vary continuously, the entire process is naturally (and generically) hysteresis-loaded.

There is no automatically functioning synchronization "mechanism" linking it to *changes* in the capacity to produce elements in Category 2 of the CCSL that is the underlying and subtle fallacy of "automatic compensation." The real meaning of "automatic compensation" as well as its very low level of probability may be illustrated by Figure 2.1 below.

Figure 2.1

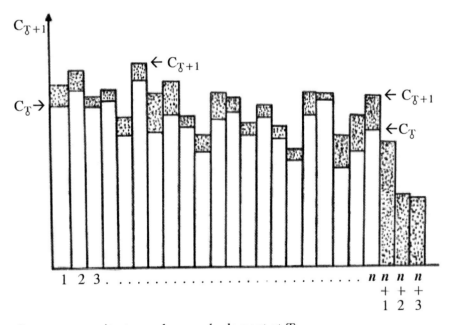

C_{Υ} = capacity to produce each element at Υ.
$C_{\Upsilon+1}$ = capacity to produce each element at $\Upsilon+1$.

Let there be *n* elements in Category 1 of the CCSL.
Let each bar represent each element of the CCSL$_{[cat. 1]}$.
Let *n* represent a commodity or service from 1, 2, 3, . . . *n* associated with each operational Telos of society (including both sectors of Omega and all categories of the CCSL).

The unshaded areas of the individual bars represent the productive capacity of each element at technological time $\mathcal{T}$.

The shaded areas represent the increase in productive capacity at technological time $\mathcal{T}+1$.

The completely shaded bars represent the commodities and services of Category 2 of the CCSL that are newly perceived candidates for incorporation, i.e., new kinds of goods and services.

Then if the theory (or "law") of automatic compensation is operational, the factors of production rendered surplus (especially labor) will be re-absorbed within a reasonable time frame after "adjustments" ("weak" form of the "law") or almost immediately as in the "strong" form of the "law." Both forms of the "Law of Automatic Compensation" go back to Ricardo, McCulloch & Mill. Mill went through a process of expressing a weak form of the law but then, conceding that the "strong" form would prevail within a reasonable time frame. For example, he at first rejects the "full auto" notion that the introduction of "machinery" as a substitute for labor will lead automatically to the reabsorption of displaced labor by way of (real) price reduction and consequent stimulation of demand. Then Mill insists at a later stage of his analysis that the substitution of "machinery" for labor will not injure the interests of the working classes, even in the short run ("strong" form) (See Appendix 6).

Referring to Figure 2.1, if McCulloch's "law" of automatic compensation was set on "full auto," so to speak, then all the shaded areas of the bars up to *n* and the completely shaded bars, shown vertically as *n*+1, *n*+2, *n*+3 (the most potent elements of Category 2 of the CCSL, in their potential for "absorbing" productive capacity added by "process innovation") corresponding to the increase in productive capacity generated between $\mathcal{T}$ and $\mathcal{T}+1$ would be reabsorbed painlessly, regardless of whether any natural limit for normal consumption had already been reached on the elements up to *n*, or whether the elements beyond *n* had been incorporated into the CCSL to any observable extent, by the discrete and contingent process of consumption accumulation described in the preceding pages. For example, if the major increases in productive capacity occurred in the agricultural/food processing industries, would this imply that consumers would bulk up to gluttonous proportions in order to "automatically" absorb the displaced labor and capital of those industries (see Appendix 7)? Or if they occurred in the armaments industries (of sector 2 of omega), would that mean an immanent build-up of personal weaponry among the civilian population corresponding to Category 2 of the CCSL and including the immediate creation, perception, and consumption of new products and services of a military nature (shaded bars beyond n)?

And would any response from consumers that falls short of "full auto" be described as a "chronic tendency" to underemployment equilibrium, or to "under-consumption"?

If "under-consumption" (a nebulous term at best) is defined with respect to the "raw" increase in capacity between τ and $\tau+1$, the answer, under the "McCullochian" dispensation (and its modern versions), would be *yes*.

But this definition of under-consumption implicitly burdens consumers (individual and institutional) with the onus of "buying up" to the full productive capacity for each and every element along the whole range of omega (CCSL and sector 2) and to almost instantaneously generate new operational teleologies into the shaded bars beyond n, and the products and services that are associated with them.

Under-consumption defined in this way completely excludes the crucial responses of consumers that are rooted *in permanently active* social, psychological and anthropological behavior. And it also neglects the crucial role of *active* time in economic behavior which is congruent with hystereses. Therefore, in terms of Telos-Technos nexus, there is no such phenomenon as "underconsumption." There is only a natural lack of correspondence between two different processes that cannot move "in phase" in a predictable deterministic fashion, except in the most episodic circumstances. And it is this neglect of time (and timing) in real economic behavior, that is the most insidious characteristic of the "law" of automatic compensation, especially in its neo-classical (subliminal) form. At least the classical economists understood that the notion of automaticity associated with "homo aeconomous's" behavior was linked in some way to his responses *in time*, which were usually described as requiring periods of "adjustment" which might require some sort of government intervention to assist displaced workers or even slow down the consequences of introducing "machinery" (Mill). But the neo-classical addiction to "path independence" precluded *any* consideration of active time in economic behavior, including the trajectory of cognitive time, which encompasses a myriad of "learning curves" with which economic behavior teems. This underlying philosophical vacancy in neo-classical analysis is almost fatal in its own right, but when the natural imperatives of human consciousness that lie behind the formation of our visible wants and their expression in economic behavior are extruded from the scope of economic thought, then there should be no real surprise at the consequent sterilization of the subject.

For the neo-classical school at least, the "law" of automatic compensation is indeed the law "that dare not speak its name."

The Ancestry of the Current Conception of the Standard of Life

The current conception of the standard of life has an eminently respectable ancestry in the classical notions of the "natural price of labor," the "price of corn," and later variations such as "conventional subsistence," the "wages fund," and the "standard of living."

These latter concepts were thought by the classical economists to tend toward physical subsistence for more or less "Malthusian" reasons, or because the real wages of labor which sustained physical sustenance were the residual of the total "pie" that the capitalists didn't get in pursuing (successfully) the "rate of exploitation" (Marx). In the use of these concepts, mass consumerism, essentially non-passive choosing in the marketplace by an enriched working class was not considered. "Workers" were considered to automatically spend up to the limits of their modest incomes and only the capitalist and rentier/landlord classes were endowed with the faculty of choice, i.e., to spend, to save, to invest, to buy "luxury" goods.

However the classical economists, especially Ricardo understood clearly that *the natural price of labor* could fluctuate considerably in the same economy and differ considerably from nation to nation even though they might be similarly endowed with natural resources and equally virtuous "laboring classes."

It was not until much later in the century that it became obvious, especially in America, that increased industrial efficiency makes it possible to procure the means of livelihood with less labor, the energies of the industrious members of the community are bent to the compassing of a higher result in conspicuous expenditure, rather than slackened to a more comfortable pace.

. . . and

as industrial efficiency increases and makes a lighter strain *possible*, the increment of output is turned to meet this want, which is indefinitely expansible after the manner commonly imputed in economic theory to the higher or spiritual wants. It is owing chiefly to the presence of this element in the standard of living that J.S. Mill was to say that "it is questionable if all the mechanical inventions yet made have lightened the toil of any human being."

—Thorstein Veblen, "The Pecuniary Standard of Living"
from *The Theory of the Leisure Class*

The Search for Veblen's Dog or The Most Immediate Ancestors of the Current Conception of the Standard of Life

The dog has advantages in the ways of uselessness as well as in special gifts of temperament . . . he has the gift of an unquestioning subservience . . . and characteristics which are of a more equivocal aesthetic value . . . He is the filthiest of the domestic animals in his person and the nastiest in his habits. . . .

—Thorstein Veblen,
The Theory of the Leisure Class,
Pecuniary Canons of Taste

Veblen's ideas are much more revealing if they are extended into an analytic trajectory that is a logical consequence of their philosophical content. Consequently, by the last quarter of the twentieth century the benefits of the "increment of output" have been offered to a much higher percentage of the population than the "leisure class" or the "predatory" financial and business classes. Therefore the majority of the consuming population is now engaged in making similar decisions about the "scale of decent consumption," "pecuniary canons of taste" . . . and the pecuniary standard of living . . . an ideal of consumption that lies just beyond our reach, or to reach which requires some strain . . . This desire is *not* guided by a rigidly invariable standard . . . the standard is flexible; and especially it is indefinitely extensible . . . It takes time for any change to permeate the mass and change the habitual attitude of the people; and especially it takes time to change the habits of those classes that are socially more remote from the radiant body.

Even the "subsistence minimum" was no longer to be considered a "rigidly determined allowance of goods, definite and invariable in kind and quantity." Veblen did not go "all the way" and simply turn "homo aeconomous" in his role of consumer, into a mere insatiability machine (J.B. Say); a poppet-valve in an "automatic compensation" engine, (J.R. McCulloch) or the choiceless victim of an imposed "rate of exploitation" in a secular passion play (Marx). Veblen, who had observed the impact of 19th century mechanical technology on the agricultural environment he was born into, grasped intuitively "the instinct of workmanship" and the requirement for efficiency and reliability that characterized economic behavior in the more or less continuous regular progress of the "industrial arts." Moreover, he had put his finger on technological change as a primal, omnipresent force acting on previously learned habits that drove observable economic behavior; but he did not regard the pressure of change in the "efficiency of industry" or "advances in technical methods . . . or in industrial organization" ("Industrial Exemption and Conservatism") as being merely exogenous "shocks" to equilibrium seeking, automatic, self-adjusting mechanisms (already the dominant "paradigm" of economic analysis by the early years of the twentieth century).

He regarded them as the primary "facts on the ground" in a modern industrial economy to which human economic behavior at both the individual level and even more importantly, at the institutional-supra level, had to adapt. It would appear, that in terms of the Telos-Technos nexus, Veblen believed intuitively that Technos led Telos, rather than both being in what would have then been termed a chicken-egg relationship—in contemporary jargon, an interactive feedback relationship.

Veblen was, in this sense, possibly the first economic thinker to consider the *base* conditions of the study of Development Economics (a change from traditional techniques and a widespread perception of the advantages to be gained by change in this most basic of all economic conditions). However in "Imperial Germany and the Industrial Revolution" (1915) Veblen reversed the arrow's direction, so to speak, and argued that Germany had an advantage over democratic states like Britain and France; because its more dominant state apparatus could channel more of the "increment of output," generated by "advances in technical methods and industrial organization" into the service of the state's war aims. In the language of this exposition Veblen was arguing that in terms of *sector* 2 of omega, Telos could lead Technos. By the same token, Veblen, a Swiftian pessimist at heart, believed that economic man, in his capacity as a consumer, would *tend toward* emulative waste, even to the extent of perversely retrenching some of the "obscurer elements of consumption" in his "canons of taste," *after* a reversal of fortune in his "external circumstances" (financial?). An especially obstinate consumer might maintain an extreme "reluctance to recede" from a certain "honorific expenditure" on household pets. But even in such changed "circumstances" the consumer exercises choice, however painfully. He is not completely at the mercy of more dominant decision-makers in the "class struggle" (Marx); nor is he an automaton, with a "marginal propensity to consume of one" and therefore abandoned to the narrowest range of economic behavior as implied in the "wages fund" debate of the classical economists. (Would such a "reluctance to recede from an accustomed standard" be condemned as a "rigidity" if it contributed to an employment decision in the labor market?)

It should be emphasized that Veblen introduced a strong qualification to his assertion that "the propensity to emulation is *probably* the strongest and most alert and most persistent of the economic *motives* proper. The "instinct of self-preservation" is stronger, and since this economic *motive* (based on Category 1 of the CCSL) will express itself in some form of economic *behavior* when some stimulus in the wider environment is perceived, another direction for consumer's behavior is possible. Moreover it is a "countervailing" tendency *toward* the frugality of fear . . . the "Savonarola" polar extreme, the primordial ancestor of J.M. Keynes' precautionary motive for holding money. Thus Veblen had clearly receded significantly from the doctrine of hyper-determinism (automaticity) in the most important form of economic behavior—consumption.

In summation, Veblen's ideas are the immediate ancestors of Omega, the operational Telos of a society, and its most important sector, the current conception of the standard of life, because:

1. He understood clearly that human economic behavior, especially consumption, was not deterministic. Veblen preferred to describe it in terms of propensities, tendencies, probabilities, etc. And he stated clearly that the "substance of the individual's *conscious* life (and by extension that of human institutions) including the "economic interest, does not lie isolated from all other interests." These words demonstrate clearly that Veblen never fell into the trap of naïve economic determinism. He was aware that societal teleologies, not normally considered "economic" (i.e., not part of the CCSL) and the goods and services associated with them, had major economic consequences . . . and that the most important of them historically was armed conflict and its equivalent "predatory" behavior in business conflict. In later chapters it will be shown that the human institution of war, precisely because it is a polar extreme of human behavior, often provides the clearest examples of the meaning and impact of traditional economic variables such as capital, work, technology, investment automaticity, insatiability, and profit and loss. Interestingly, even the mercilessly criticized concept of the "wages fund," so dear to the hearts of the classical economists, has a much clearer meaning in a war Telos, e.g., rationing, military-issue, wages-goods, and standard commodities.

2. Veblen stated in the language of his own time that economic man acted along the trajectory of his own history . . . that he was a profoundly *path dependent* creature. Although he sometimes carried this point to anthropological extremes, he repeatedly invoked the importance of learned habits, their persistence through time, time to respond to *changing* stimuli, the *timing* of economic behavior (hardly automatic in Veblen's view) and the "process of unfolding" that lies behind *conspicuous* economic behavior. These are hardly the sort of ideas that lead to "path independence," unexplained factor endowments, "given" menus of commodities to *determine* utility "fields" and "pseudo production functions" (refer to the late Joan Robinson, et al.)

3. Veblen understood that many elements in the "pecuniary standard of living" (essentially Categories 1 and 2[1] of the CCSL) were not "existential imperatives" . . . only teleological perceptions of the wider environment that were relevant to consumption decisions at a par-

ticular time, and in particular societies, and within their constituent peer groups. (Recall Alfred North Whitehead's concept of "the Teleological aim at some future ideal" or "the conceptual anticipation of the future.") He saw clearly how incomplete the vision of economic man as an heuristic, rational decision maker really was . . . and how little it really explained. Nor did he believe that "homo aeconomous" was mechanically destined for such a role by the inexorable grinding away of a Walrasian, perfectly competitive market-clearing machine. Indeed this is the very "paradigm" that needs the myth of unrestrained insatiability (or the infinite desire for commodities) as its own existential imperative. Veblen's explanation of consumers' behavior can live without it.

Instead, he created a much more plausible model of consumption behavior which was heterogeneous, (included the irrational, which itself produced economic events of irreversible consequence) and which was far more disturb*ing* in its responses to stimuli than disturb*ed* by them. In effect, it was a model far more amenable to further development than the theoretical and empirical dead end of utility theory. It is small criticism that Veblen located far too much of that disturb*ing* (his word for contingent) behavior in the business and financial "classes" of his day. They were probably no different than their counterparts a century later—just far fewer, and hence more conspicuous. But Veblen's ideas were a breath of fresh air from the crack-pot determinism of certain of his predecessors, and from the more disguised version that was rapidly developing among some of his contemporaries.

If Veblen had lived into the "golden age" of neo-classical "path independence," he would have surely remarked on the resemblance between Utility as a "field in commodity space" and the cargo cults that arose among the natives of Borneo, New Guinea and other more remote islands of the South Pacific in the aftermath of World War II.

After American forces abandoned huge stores of food, vehicles, fuel, clothing, ammunition, etc., the residents of the islands continued to wait in vain for the ships and airplanes of the recent past to bring in their precious cargos, just as they had once done on an almost daily basis, i.e., for their "unexplained" factor endowments" and "virtual" commodities that had appeared from the skies. When they failed to materialize, the local shamans "set up shop" inside the hulks of abandoned ve-

hicles and airplane fuselages and engaged in appropriate worship by rotating manually the aerials of departed radios and radar sets. This was
often accompanied by chanting and songs of varied origin.

It would be an interesting exercise in futility to try and "aggregate"—
or functionally relate in any way—the theories of individuals' utility and
ordered preference to the ideas in this chapter. The impossibility of doing so in an economically meaningful way is a direct consequence of the
gestalt nature of the subject.

Appendices to Chapter 2

Appendix 1

The current conception of the standard may be clarified further if it is "visualized" in the following Venn Diagram: (The general idea is to minimize the number of "empty" sets.)

The Current Conception of The Standard of Life at Time ♈

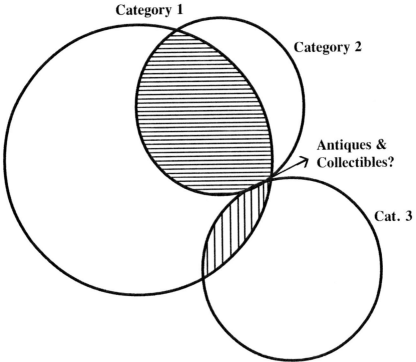

The horizontally hatched area common to both 1 and 2 represents those elements which are physically present in the existent "standard of living" to a certain "measurable" extent, but are capable of being consumed to a greater extent, both quantitatively and qualitatively and are influencing economic behavior in that direction. They may be thought of as those elements whose increased consumption would be a benefit of the income and substitution of effects because their quantity is not yet deemed to have reached "saturation" levels—for example, refrigerators and freezers, circa 1960; television sets, about 1965; personal computers in the mid-nineteen nineties.

The unshaded area of Category 2 represents very approximately those elements which are new *kinds* of products; that is, they are involved in the phenomenon known as "product innovation" at time T. This does not necessarily imply that such product innovation will be successful—merely that is affecting at least some observable economic behavior in that direction at T (e.g. "Autonomous" investment). But this sub-set of Category 2 of the CCSL is presumably the most potent in its ability to *absorb* the additional productive capacity of "process innovation." The vertically hatched area can be thought of as obsolescent elements in the standard of living, such as horse-drawn transportation in the nineteen twenties or what many current ('90's) models of PC's will be in the early years of the 21st century when voice or plain hand-written-activated computers will replace any of the current models. It may also be interpreted as so called "fad" elements, in the fashion and entertainment industries. The point at which circles representing categories 1, 2, and 3 meet could be interpreted as antiques and collectibles. It may also represent elements whose participation in Category 1 may be subsiding, but are not necessarily headed for (total) obsolescence. Other configurations can be constructed by the reader—for example, the military weapons component of sector 2 of Omega. How might its intersection with Category 2 be interpreted when some governments were divesting themselves of their old "cold war" inventory?

Appendix 2

One of the more over-wrought arguments for the indisputable existence of "insatiability of demand," while seeming to decry it, was Tibor Scitovsky's "The Joyless Economy" (1976). "Any achievement no matter how impressive, is quickly overlooked in favor of new *unquenched* demands. Move into a new house and it will give *you* satisfaction for only a short while; within a few *months you* will want a bigger house or a cottage . . . or a faster car." This rather moralistic, pseudo-scientific argument is, of course, just another way of saying that the consumer will always, automatically and *compulsively,* absorb any conceivable increase in productive capacity. Poor chap! He just can't help it. Besides, this is a valuable attribute of human nature for those whose "field" theories of consumer behaviors (with static choice of commodities and path independence) cannot exist without it. J. B. Say, McCulloch, Walras, et al, said it with more brevity and less moralizing.

Appendix 3

A sort of historical "evolution" takes place in the shape (curvature) of demand curves for those commodities (and services) which are in the unshaded area of Category 2 of the diagram in Appendix 1. (Product innovation). The following *hypothetical* presentation should be visualized as unfolding in three stages corresponding to a gradually declining threshold of consumption: $\theta_1 > \theta_2 > \theta_3$

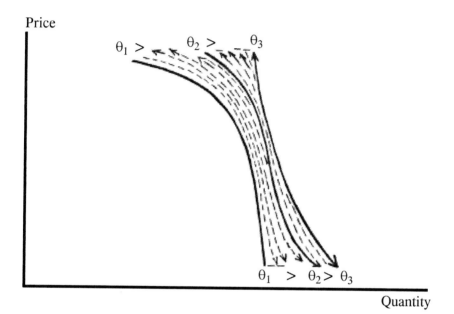

Price

$\theta_1 > \qquad \theta_2 > \qquad \theta_3$

$\theta_1 \quad > \quad \theta_2 > \theta_3$

Quantity

Demand for a new kind of commodity or service entering the CCSL (as the result of product innovation) is very *fragile* in terms of elasticity, especially for price increases, during the "trial and decision" period, θ_1. By the same token, a high elasticity will prevail as a response to a significant price decrease. The curve gradually becomes less fragile as it evolves into a "normally" integrated element of the CCSL, where the θ barrier has been irrevocably "cleared" by more and more consumers. By the time the "life cycle" of the commodity has matured (θ_3), elasticities are far more stable, i.e., major price reductions resulting from increases in productivity will no longer result in "absorption" of excess capacity to the same extent as "saturation" of the market is approached—a sort of "whiplash" effect visually.

Appendix 4

The generation of quantity of variety in the distinct elements of the CCSL is not automatic, nor insatiably and "ergodically" consumed in perfect phase with their generation by the aggregate of "representative" consumers. The interaction between commodity creation and the reactive behavior of consumers is of a contingent nature, and hysteresis-loaded. It cannot be described by linear, deterministic models of consumers' behavior . . . or fed into such models as "dummy" commodity variables, for reasons of "analytic tractability," to accomodate the dubious construct of "the representative consumer." Such is the nature of "events" in category two of the CCSL. The qualitative descriptions of what ordinary human-beings like to buy, the ebb and flow of their choices, are what makes the subject interesting, as the great Karl Menger understood more than a century ago . . . and which posturing "moralists" like Scitovsky and John Kenneth Galbraith unlearned during the 20th century.

The threshold of consumption finds real expression in the social fate of consumers whose "q barrier" lowers more than is considered appropriate following a rise from modest levels of income or economic status. The dictionary of vituperation has provided a more than adequate repertoire of idioms on their behalf—"nouveaux riches," "parvenue," "n—er rich," "social climbers," . . . "pushy," . . . "flashy," etc. By the same token, and under similar circumstances, the "q barrier" may become infinitely high for some perfectly respectable commodities and services if they are associated in the consumer's mind with a group or lifestyle that the consumer now regards with great disdain. Snob appeal produces economic behavior (example: switching children from publically funded to fee-based private schools, i.e., from *Sector* 2 of Telos to *Category* 2 of CCSL.

Appendix 5

In very general terms the critical increment for a product x in Category 2 of the CCSL, with n elements in Category 1 of the CCSL is given by:

$$\Delta Y_{\bar{0}}^{x} = \frac{1}{w}\{\Delta w\} + \left\{ \sum_{i=1}^{n} \pm \frac{(r_{i}\Delta v_{i})}{P_{i}} \right\} = \theta_{x}^{T} P_{x}^{T}$$

where Δw = change in money income received
w = initial level of money income received
Δv_{i} = the change in money value of the ith element in Category 1 of the CCSL.
r_{i} = the (percentage) weight of w spent on the ith element of Category 1 of the CCSL
P_{i} = the initial price of i

Providing there *exists* such a commodity x that can "trigger" a particular change in real income to "transform" into the critical increment for Product x.

Thus, this particular "model" of consumption accumulation is inherently contingency loaded, rather than in the nature of "automatic compensation" or a consequence of "insatiability" or an "infinite demand for commodities." The consumer is considered to be a random chooser of products and services in Category 2 of the CCSL. He may choose *none* at a particular Technological time, *or* some, *or* even be in a state such that "a fresh advance in conspicuous expenditure is relatively easy; indeed it takes place *almost* as a matter of course" (Veblen).

Appendix 6

Ricardo also did not consider the "machinery question" to be settled. In the third edition of his "principles" he administered something of a jolt to contemporary economists who had also considered the question, and closed it by assuming "automaticity and insatiability." Ricardo introduced the possibility that there could really exist "injury to workers' interests" from the introduction of "machinery." But Ricardo meanders back to the automatic compensators by insisting that all such "injurious" effects could be avoided, *if* "machinery" were financed out of previous earnings. He also admits that the demand for workers' labor would be reduced for a "considerable interval" . . . *of time*. Thus, it would appear that Ricardo had at one point switched from believing that "gluts were impossible, logically, to fearing that they were possible because "capitalists" would in fact change more and more "circulating capital," all of which was used to pay workers into "fixed" capital—or "machinery"—which tended to displace workers.

Displaced workers greatly exceeded the number of workers used to make the "machinery;" there was an underlying assumption, even in Ricardo's day, that the machine tool industry was much less labor intensive than the "wages goods" industries. Also, Ricardo seems to have believed that even *un*displaced workers would not enjoy a sufficient increase (if any) in their wages to participate in the benefits of income effects. Therefore, they were not effective absorbers of increased capacity, but could be engaged in some alternative employment via the luxurious lifestyles of those who exercised the choices arising from the income effects of "machinery."

Appendix 7

This would certainly be he ultimate, surrealistic expression of the income effect. Would it trigger a "return to the land"?

Appendix 8

By the same token, there are *technical* limits to the bargaining power of particular unions to "hold their own." *If* the content and rate of flow of Technological time (see Chapter 3), determined by the relative presence of "ideal and "artisan-incremental" technologies, had reduced the number of stages of production in that particular sector, then the "ultimate sanction" (J S. Mill) of the market-correction system would bring them "down to earth" by determining the real value of their particular kind of labor, as a commodity at a particular technological time. In this case, the flow of technological time would determine prices, regardless of the degree of imperfect competition.

Appendix 9

The reader should be reminded of a classic statement about the economic behavior of an individual consumer in a perfect timeless "circular flow" (i.e., Say's law) economy, by Joseph Schumpeter in Chapter I of *The Theory of Economic Development*, p. 52, Galaxy Book, Oxford University Press, 1961, Redvers Opie translation.

> For every individual values his money income really, according to the goods which he actually obtains with it. . . . When he speaks of the value of money, the range of goods he customarily purchases floats more or less plainly before his eyes.

In Chapter 4, the fateful connection between the "timelessness" of Say's law, exogenous Technos, and the "straitjacket" of the equilibrium "paradigm" will be covered in more detail.

The reader should consider Alfred Marshall's inadvertent but penetrating denial of consumer insatiability, the underlying human behavioral pattern embodied by McCulloch's "Law" of automatic compensation: "(Wo)men can have the power to purchase, but may not choose to use it." The reader should also consult Samuel Butler, the eminent Victorian anti-Utopian (Erewhon), who entertained similar sentiments.

Summary of Content of Chapter 2

. . . and why it is distinct and incompatible with all contemporary and competing "paradigms" about consumers' behavior, or, Opening up the composition of Consumer demand to authentic dynamic analysis:

We have introduced here a "petit-teleologie"/decision threshold theory (in the spirit of Wittgenstein's image-building) of change in the composition of consumer demand. We have not chosen to

1. Bury it under a mountain of impenetrable aggregates as in the Keynesian "consumption function,"
2. Render it invisible under that opaque rubric of "consumers' tastes held constant," or
3. Simply throw up our hands with the futile lament of "Where can we even begin!" and

4. "We don't have to worry at all about what goes on inside the belly of that beast. It's just typical 'ergodic' behavior anyway;" or in our terms, "automatically compensating" in perfect phase with improvements in manufacturers' productivity of consumer-commodities.

Note the unmistakable resemblance of this mode of "artful-dodging" to the treatment of technology as an automatic (or "ergodic"—Paul Davidson's immortal phrase) "cargo-cult" rescuer from any impact at all on the natural environment; or the inexhaustible availability of "taken-for-granted" infinitely substitutable input resources; the baleful and inevitable consequence of treating our all-too-human Promethean behavior as an exogenous "shock," a residual operator, an externality, or total banishment to the underworld of "ceteris-parabus"!

It should be noted that all of these analytic stratagems completely sidestep the inevitable interactive gestalt nature of consumers' behavior as it "morphs" into its aggregate societal effects, which cannot be simply added up "arithmomorphically" (Georgescu-Roegen's phrase) in the interests of "analytic-tractability." This dilemma obviously cries out for a gestalt mode of connectivity, from the subjective individual (or micro level of human behavior) to the social aggregate called *consumption*— the observable and fascinating materiality of our human "hedonistic" drives. Therefore any gestalt mode of description requires a concise (not precise) qualitative description of the distinct elements of consumption (analysis of differences in kind and heterogeneity, quantity of variety, et al) before we can proceed to an authentic quantitative analysis of change in the composition of hedonistically-oriented consumption. In other words, we cannot deploy immediately all the typically positivist tricks of spurious quantifiability, in the interests of "analytic tractability." All this achieves is to "teach away" from the true principles of human economic behavior. We have at least "started the ball rolling." See especially Appendices 1 to 5 of Chapter Two.

Suggestions for Further Investigation

In his consideration of the role of "complexity" in the economic process (*not* "system"),the great Karl Manger was always fascinated by the proliferation—the "comings and goings"—of new kinds of commodities. (See Appendices 1, 3, and 5 of this chapter). That is, Category 2 of the current conception of the standard of life—CCSL. This relates to the concept of "quantity of variety" and "distinct elements," as described by the "cyberneticist" Ross Ashby in the 1950s. This subject also intrigued Charles Babbage of "calculating-engine" fame who discussed it in *The Economy of Machinery and Manufactures*, 1832 edition, Chapter 24, "Over Manufacturing" and with his friend John Stuart Mill.

Note

1. This understanding is implicit in the existence of Category 3 of the CCSL to especially vertically hatched area of Venn Diagram (see Appendix 1).

Chapter Three

Technos, Technological Time, or The Promethean Imperative

Prometheus, the creator of Mankind . . . the wisest of his race and Athene, at whose birth from Zeus's head he had assisted, taught him Architecture, Astronomy, Mathematics, Navigation, Medicine, and other *useful* arts, which he passed on to Mankind. But Zeus . . . grew angry at their *increasing* talents and powers.

On his (Prometheus's) arrival at Olympus . . . he lighted a torch the fiery chariot of the sun and presently broke from it a fragment of glowing charcoal, which he thrust into the pithy hollow of a fennel stalk. Then, extinguishing his torch he stole away undiscovered and gave fire to Mankind.

> —Robert Graves, *The Greek Myths*, Volume One, 39.c - 39.h; Braziller Inc. 1959 Edition.

. . . he is possessed of a taste for effective work, and a distaste for futile effort. He has a sense of the merit of serviceability or *efficiency* and of the demerit of futility, waste or incapacity. This aptitude or propensity may be called the *instinct* of *workmanship*. . . .

> —Thorstein Veblen, *Theory of the Leisure Class*, Chapter 1

Other circumstances permitting, that instinct (of workmanship) disposes men to look with favor upon productive efficiency and on whatever is of human *use*. . . . The instinct of workmanship is present in all men, and asserts itself even under very adverse circumstances. So that however wasteful a given expenditure may be in reality, it must at least have some colorable excuse *in the way of an ostensible purpose*. . . .

So long as all labor continued to be performed exclusively by slaves, the baseness of all productive effort was too constantly and deterrently present in the mind of men to allow the instinct of workmanship seriously to take effect in the direction of industrial usefulness.

—Thorstein Veblen,
Conspicuous Consumption, Chapter 4

If all significant macro-economic change is only expressed in terms of shifting levels of equilibrium states, then this paradigm (no matter to what levels of analytic sophistication it presumes) has only succeeded in extruding any notion of active time from economic thought. Analysis based on the equilibrium construct is therefore the true heir to an authentic Say's "law" economy, the contemporary spouse of McCulloch's theory of "automatic compensation," and the true son of Walras's determinate market equilibrium. Consequently, this kind of paradigm can only treat economically viable technological change as a discontinuity between shifting equilibrium states. Treating Technos as a discontinuity is tantamount to treating it as a potential *shock* force, like fault lines in the earth's crust; but a "shock" is the most extreme form of intrusive force. Therefore equilibrium analysis, as the offspring of the most extreme form of determinism (perfect automaticity in human economic behavior), approaches magic in its implications. It causes action at a distance with no knowledge of the connective temporal and spatial events. Its analogue in neo-classical analysis is the notion of technology as a "field" in factor-input space in order to provide *automatic* symmetry with the older notion of utility as a "field" in commodity space. Thus the trajectory of economic history is cut off from what Veblen thought was the primal force in economics: changes in the efficiency of production technology and in the range of goods and services it *offers* to consumers act as a stimulus to their response as potential buyers. Indeed, when the logical outcome of equilibrium's domination of the subject has been to treat one of the two primal motivations of economic behavior as a "shock," then the most real has been consigned to the status of an outsider, and the purely artificial has become that which is "real"; truly a *reductio ad absurdam*.

In the simplest possible terms, what does an advance in technology of the factors of production actually do?

It enables society to use its existing inventory of labor, natural resources, and the various forms of capital more efficiently. This can be expressed in a number of ways:

1. It increases the output of goods and services with the *same* quantity of work during an interval of chronological time that is equal to that of a comparable preceding period.
2. It creates new alternative processes that use hitherto underutilized resources and factors of production. This is, it creates additions to the existing inventories of technologies that in total constitute the "state of the art." (Technologies are themselves composed of techniques, and techniques consist of a *unique* "bundle" of skills, material, equipment, and organization, etc.)

A related statement that also has operational meaning is this: An increase in the productive power of Technos—with natural resources held constant—is equivalent to a discovery of a new source of natural resources with the existing state of the art held constant. These points should be compared with Schumpeter's classic statement of the "five cases" that are "covered" by the "concept of economic development" and "new combinations that *may* in time grow out of the old by continuous adjustment in small steps. . . . (Chapter II of *The Theory of Economic Development*, Oxford University Press, 1961, Galaxy Book). At the conclusion of this chapter, more will be said about current trends in the *abuse* of Schumpeter's explanation of "new combinations of productive means."

3. Progress in the technology of production allows a *smaller* quantity of work to produce the *same* output of goods and services in an *equal* interval of chronological time. Statements one and three can be transformed into:
4. An advance in the technology of production allows the same output of goods and services to be produced by the *same* quantity of work in a *smaller* interval of chronological time.

In statement 1, neither the quantity of work nor the interval of chronological time changes because there is built into it (unobtrusively) McCullochian automaticity, as a kind of "bottom line"—a hope disguised as an assumption that the old level of the quantity of work will be *conserved*—in terms of this exposition, by consumers' action via Categories 1 and 2 of the CCSL.

But in statement three, advances in the technology of production are *compressing* the *quantity of work required* to be defined in Chapter Four as the *natural participation rate*. And in statement four, an advance in the technology of production is said to *compress chronological time*, i.e., in this case the conventional or average time span of a "normal" working day that prevails in a particular economy.

The statement that is of primary and practical importance in terms of the most widely accepted policy goals is number one: economic man almost universally chooses the rewards of a full working day over the consequences of a compressed one, which would be equivalent to choosing more leisure time. The conclusion to be reached from the previous material is fairly evident. Any useful definition of the role of Technos must convey an understanding that economically viable activity *is* the content of economic time. Field- and equilibrium-based economic theory simply consigns the role of time to inactive "clock" time between periods of adjustment that are either fast (short run) or uncertain (long run) in their paths to market-clearing equilibrium states . . . or lead inevitably to entrenched and hidden fallacies such as the widespread misconception that there is a one-to-one correspondence between progress in technology and the flow of chronological time. The *lack* of *automatic* correspondence between the two is the "stuff" of economic and technological history . . . and the history of conflict (see Appendix 1).

The consequences of change in Technos must be directly and systemically linked to the quantity of work that is *naturally* required through active, event-laden time, at the macro-economic level, without getting caught in the cul-de-sac of aggregation problems that are essentially insoluble in a subject that is governed largely by gestalt relationships.

A logical consequence of developing an operational description of technological change ought to be a subsuming of vague and confusing dichotomies such as "long run" vs. "short run"; substitution vs. pure technical "innovation"; accumulation of (constant vintage?) capital vs. Technical advance as contributors to "steady state equilibrium growth paths"; "high" technology and low (?) technology, and so on.

The Willful Liquidation of Active time in Neo-classical Analysis and Its Persistent Consequences

"We live in an age where the obvious needs constant repetition"
—George Orwell

No amount of stretching or manipulating of "path-independent" (and/or) equilibrium *based*) conceptualizing can represent the role of time in economic thought without sinking into a notoriously well-criticized morass of contradictions, inconsistencies and just plain false assumptions. This is equivalent to a systemic inability to deal with Technos. Consider Figure 3.1, below:

Figure 3.1

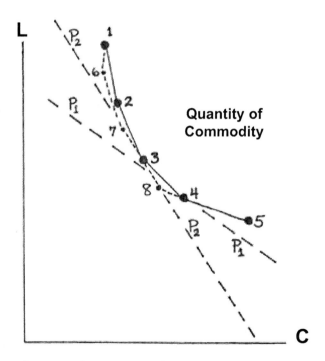

"C" along the horizontal axis represents CAPITAL—homogeneous.
"L" along the vertical axis represents LABOR—homogeneous.
The Isoquant above is the well-known field representation of technology in input space (appropriately condensed to C and L).

It represents all *given* combinations of capital and labor that are capable of producing quantity Q of a certain commodity; all possible cost environments are *"given"* in various slopes of price lines, $p_1 \ldots p_2 \ldots$ $p_3 \ldots$ i.e., in terms of one price—the ratios of "C" to "L". The *choice* of a particular combination of the two factors of production (activity) depends on the prevailing one-price ratio. When the "one price" line and the isoquant are tangential, the "activity" choice that is an element of the "technology" are in some sort of "equilibrium"; e.g., that activity, represented by point 4, produces quantity Q of the commodity. A "least cost" match has been made.

One rational response from the *relevant industry* (micro-economic domain) is to *develop* additional techniques (6, 7, 8) as in 3-1, in order to cope with *reasonably foreseeable change* in the cost environment that is most relevant to the industry and its component firms. This turns the isoquant representing the *inventory* of techniques, comprising the technology for producing quantity Q of a *particular* commodity, into a sort of cumulative industry learning curve.

The isoquant becomes more and more smoothly curved, representing the increasing flexibility of the industry's productive technology for making the particular product, which may be one of many in that industry. It also appears to validate *substitution* as a perfectly natural form of technological change in process innovation. Indeed, any concept of inventory includes the process of "turn-over" or "flow-through" as valid measures of change. Can we therefore infer that the ebb and flow of techniques along a gradually smoothing learning curve of *substitution* activities is, in itself, sufficient to represent technological change in production innovation? Indeed, in the light of the preceding material, we might well question the perversity of a "paradigm" that actually excludes substitution (along *given* "production functions") as a valid expression of technological change. How can the process of adding, modifying and re-cycling the inter-related techniques of which maturing technologies are composed (see Appendix 13) and the very substance of creative adaptability in human economic behavior be "exogenous" to any useful mode of economic analysis (see Appendix 2)? In this respect, the field metaphor and the equilibrium "paradigm" have excluded the rich literature of economic and technological history, the very stuff of the Promethean imperative and the art of economic viability, from the domain of analysis; one more *reductio ad absurdum* debited to their account, and a clear illustration of how the exclusion of active time in the form most appropriate to economics (technological time) is equivalent to the exclusion of technological change from economic analysis (see Appendix 16).

It is also obvious how a cumulative industry learning curve approach— culminating in a representation of technology as a semi-continuum of techniques which may be substituted for one another as adaptations to changing cost environments—is taboo in the equilibrium-cum-field metaphor of the neo-classical paradigm: It expresses technological change as an irreversible evolutionary process *active* time; not just "given" as a "free good"; the insidious but subliminal dead-end to which the equilibrium and "field" metaphors ultimately led.

However, in the context of a Telos-Technos explanation of economic activity, evolving technology may be quite naturally and unambiguously expressed as a kind of substitution along *evolving* (pseudo) production functions, not *given* ones. Of course, one has to believe in the existence of "production functions" as well as in the existence of "capital" as a defined homogeneous, technical unit that can be compared and "measured" from one economic era to another. This leads to a whole other inconsistent and unmanageable set of assumptions.

Suppose there occurs a more or less, not unnatural shift in the cost environment, with which the firm or industry is *not* experienced. Which "activity" is the economically viable one? What is its economic interpretation in terms of the isoquants (equivalent to "fixed" technical coefficients) that are the most important geometrical construct of the field metaphor technology?

Consider Figure 3.2 on the following page. One way of attempting to describe the adaptation to this changed cost environment is to draw two isoquants, showing the ability to produce the *same* quantity Q of a particular commodity at technological times T_1 and T_2.

In this representation, a shift in technological time (improvement in the productive power of capital and labor) results in the ability to produce the same quantity Q of a commodity with lesser "amounts" of capital and labor ensembles at each and every corresponding point along the two field representations of the production function.

This representation *seems* to clarify the ideal differentiation between real improvement in the economies of production technology and mere substitution along given production functions. But second thoughts about it reveal something even worse than all the sloppily concealed philosophical underpinnings of an unshakeable belief in the existence of production functions (e.g., unit homogeneity of capital and labor, invari-

Figure 3.2

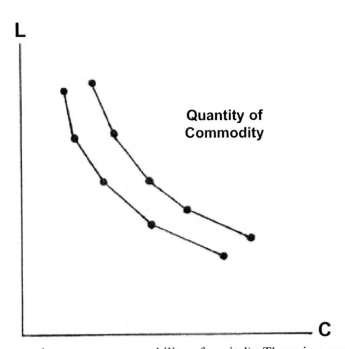

ance of factor endowments, measurability of capital). There is a complete loss of the sense of active economic time and its connection with evolutionary development of the industry. After all, this representation implies strongly that all techniques from T_1 have been completely abandoned or lost and that the cost environment that was once the cause of their "best practice" status has ceased to have any probability of recurrence, i.e., two technological times that do not share a single technique in common in that particular industry. This is highly improbable to say the least or it represents a "long run" perspective so remote that it constitutes a *total* discontinuity in a major form of human collective behavior . . . a sort of economic/technological amnesia. Yet it satisfies the criteria for authentic technological progress in the timeless, path-independent world of the neo-classical "paradigm." All that is required is that we surrender the real empirical observation that economic behavior (in producing goods and services) has a supporting cognitive history that is, for all practical considerations, irreversible; in return for a blind faith in the timeless production function—the equivalent of believing in technology as a "free good" . . . a "field in factor endowment space."

    Undaunted by our previous attempts to stretch the "timeless" equilibrium-based, and pseudo-quantitative "paradigm" of the neo-classical school into a truly dynamic (active time) and revealing description of economic events, let us consider the following Figures, 3.3, 3.4, and 3.5;

Figure 3.3

Π represents output per unit of labor
C represents "quantity of capital" per unit of labor

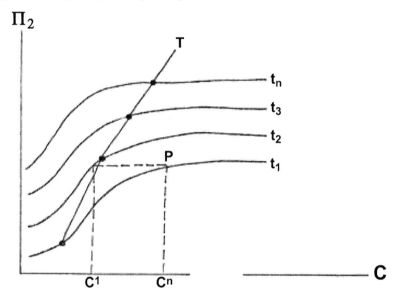

The curves t_1, t_2, t_3, t_4, . . . t_n represent the value of Π when increasing amounts of capital per unit of labor are applied within the same technological time. Within each "t" there is a point reached where any further application of *constant vintage* capital is futile in increasing the marginal productivity of labor. This case reflects a kind of technological lock-in where the possibility of competition demanding an earlier leap to a "higher" technology is disregarded in favor of squeezing out the last dollar of cost-benefit from the existing "constant vintage" capital. These figures not only imply that there exists a homogeneous technical measure of capital that is comparable through time (convincingly argued against by Piero Sraffa) but that the various forms of inventory can somehow be fused into a single timeless homogeneous unit and somehow be separated into "vintages" of such capital units, and then "aggregated" along a continuum; and that the contribution to gross productivity by purely technical innovation can somehow be separated out from that of brute accumulation of constant vintage "units" of capital. It also raises some very serious "embodiment" issues whose resolution would require several eons of near theological acrimony.

If we accept all the previous assumptions embedded or explicit in the neo-classical paradigm, then Figure 3.3 represents the case where the industry or firm moves on to a new technological time at the point where constant returns to scale changes into diminishing returns to scale in the application of measurable units of constant vintage capital to homogeneous labor (another dubious concept that simultaneously obfuscates the concept of human capital and denies the reality of path dependent cognitive time, both of which are implicit in the concept of technological time - $\mathcal{T}$) This, of course amounts to waiting to the last possible moment to declare the existing technology obsolete and headed for scrapping. It also implies that improved technology is more or less entirely embodied (and its value captured) in successively newer equipment and machinery, and that there is a more or less one-to-one correspondence between the appearance of such "machinery" through chronological time and technological progress.

This subliminal oversimplification of Technos ignores the heterogeneity of physical capital as to vintage, retrofits, and modifications (See Appendix 6), state of human skills, varying types and ages of inventory in the pipe-line, social infrastructure, transportation networks and the like—all *co-existing,* interacting and intertwined with one another in a seemingly anarchic, bewildering and untraceable manner—only to result in a rational and timely supply of all those goods and services that lead to the providing of the current conception of the standard of life. Only a concept such as technological time, which "black-boxes" these myriad interactions instead of attempting to "dis-aggregate" them into packages of spurious "quantifiables" can clarify their impact and valuation at the *macro*-economic level and on the traditional economic variables such as employment, work, capital, investment and consumption.

Thus the concept of technological time ($\mathcal{T}$) is the most appropriate gestalt concept for economics. The futile gropings of the neo-classical practitioners over the past half-century almost cry out for it in spite of themselves—because all the heterogeneous attributes, events, and textures of economic life cannot be aggregated to it, nor can spurious quantification of any one of the traditional economic variables capture it (see Appendix 13).

Figure 3.4

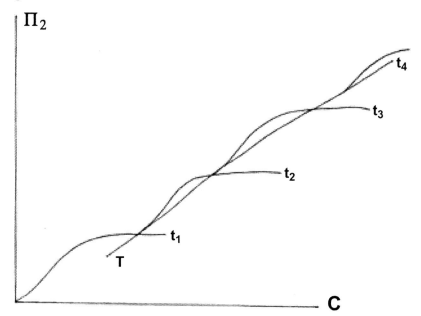

Figure 3.5

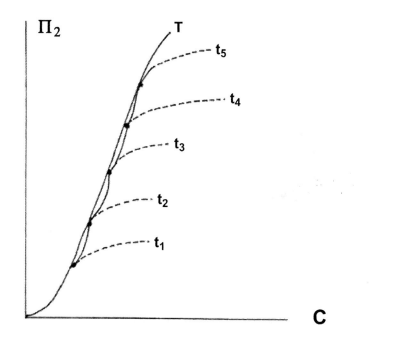

Similarly, Figure 3.4 represents a slower pace of change in Υ than in Figure 3.3 because the curves are further apart and the firm or industry does not move on to a new "technological time" until *all* the potential of the previous one is exhausted, i.e., the "hit in" or scrapping time is postponed.

The most extreme case is illustrated in Figure 3.5 if it is stipulated that the firm or industry moves on to a new technological time exactly when it reaches the point where constant returns replaces increasing returns to scale. In this case, the Υ curve becomes considerably steeper and embraces the curves from the top. Figure 3.5 may be interpreted as a case of breakneck speed of technological development possibly fueled by hyper-competitiveness in the perception of the CCSL or by military competition (Appendix 3), e.g., the Battle of the Atlantic during World War II, in which both electronic and information retrieval technology (Ultra vs. Enigma) often achieved major advances in a matter of months that would have normally taken years in peace-time—a classic case of Telos leading Technos instead of Technos driving Telos (refer back to Chapter 2, *Imperial Germany and the Industrial Revolution*, 1915, Veblen). The reader could experiment with various forms and parameters of the preceding curves. But they amount to little more than empirically hollow descriptions of technological change, precisely because they have built into them the underlying neo-classical assumptions of (spurious) quantifiability, and technology as a "free good." Such assumptions obscure rather than enlighten. But the preceding material does point the way toward what is really needed in a *gestalt*-oriented description of Technos—*a taxonomic approach and a "cut" concept* that is applicable in an economic context, so that at least we are aware of the boundaries within which some degree of quantifiability and valuation is possible, and beyond which the principle of quantification is either spurious or is being abused.

Technological Time—What is It?
What Will it Achieve in a More Fully Developed Form That is Not Possible Within the Neo-classical Straitjacket?

When technology is treated as an *omnipresent*, natural expression of human economic behavior (individual and collective) instead of a "shock" outside the conventional boundaries of traditional variables, then active, irreversible, evolutionary time imposes itself as a normal and unavoidable ingredient on the subject. As will be shown in a later chapter, it also will enable us to derive a true Schumpeterian economics of development, without making development synonymous with "growth," or saddling mankind with a blind hope that technology will, like a cargo cult, somehow automatically rescue us from the consequences of irreversible damage to the natural environment (see Appendix 4). For convenience and brevity, the latter historical case will be referred to as the "passenger pigeon scenario." But it is no longer a cause of puzzlement how a blind faith in the existence of production functions, path independent field metaphors and even the most updated versions of the equilibrium paradigm (e.g., "rest points in decision space" and multiple equilibrium states) have led to a cavalier disregard of the passenger pigeon scenario, even among otherwise rational thinkers on the subject.

Any solution to the dead-end conundrum of neo-classical economics must lead to a concept of active cognitive time that cannot be derived from equilibrium or field-based concepts, which are path independent— that is, *timeless*. And this is precisely the function of technological time, $\mathfrak{T}$, in a Telos-Technos explanation of economic history, i.e., real economic time. When complemented by its complex interaction with Telos, it also allows for *non*-economic imperatives to be a cause of observable economic history rather than be simplistically determined or even subsumed by "purely economic forces," whatever that has ever meant. In doing so, it incorporates into its meaning Veblen's profound insight that economic behavior should never be considered in isolation from non-economic modes of human behavior. (refer back to Chapter 2) . . . insights that he shared with others such as Tawney and Weber . . . but which are even more incomprehensible to Marxists than they are to the neo-classical school.

In the remainder of this chapter we shall at least begin to develop the concept of technological time as a solution to the false duality of the "short run" vs. the "long run" and to at last address Schumper's insight that economics in its present stage of development falls short of becoming a truly "historical" or evolutionary subject because "it is not possible to explain economic change by previous economic conditions alone." Or . . .

economic theory in the traditional sense contributes next to nothing when it comes to . . . making development or the historical outcome of it intelligible, by working out the *elements* which characterize a situation or determine an issue.

or . . .

static analysis is not only unable to predict the consequences of discontinuous change in the traditional way of doing things (as in "fixed technical coefficients"). It can neither explain the occurrence of such productive revolutions nor the phenomenon which accompany them (which we have explained here as being rooted in the Promethean imperative—Technos). It can only *investigate the new equilibrium position* after the changes have occurred.

—Chapter II of the *Theory of Economic Development*, Oxford University Press, 1961 edition

The virgin soil ploughed up by Schumpeter has remained fallow for much too long. This hiatus in economic theory cannot be wished away by proclamations of automatic complementarity with neo-classical (or Keynesion) equilibrium theory, nor with futile exaggerations of new-found power in the equilibrium paradigm, e.g., equilibrium as a "rest point in the space of decision rules" which can somehow give economists the conceptual framework to analyze environments in which dynamics and uncertainty play central roles.

The most important role of technological time ($\mathcal{T}$) is to act as a truly historical, time-path dependent vehicle of economic events, that unifies rather than obscures the flow of causation and consequence in economic thought. Consequently, it may be useful for the reader to envisage $\mathcal{T}$ as an "operator" acting upon the most important economic variables ("operands") (see Appendix 13) such as the various forms of capital, labor, the CCSL, natural resources, the quality of the environment and the like. Although there is no suggestion that this line of thought can ever be developed in a mathematically rigorous fashion within an economic context, it will become evident as we move along that certain constructs that have emerged as analytic "tools" during the past half century (capital vintage, embodiment concepts, rigorous separation of growth into that portion caused by "technological" innovation and that caused by quantitative accumulation of "capital" et al) will appear to become redundant, as the process tends to resemble more and more a kind of 'Occam's Razor" (see Appendix 5). Transformations will, in consequence, occur and these will be described with a somewhat altered terminology, such as the Natural Participation Rate (Chapter 4), Degenerate Income Levels, annihilation of capital values, "Ideal Technologies," labor generated as a "free good," short-term gain vs. passenger pigeon trade-offs, (a scenario that denies faith in Technos as a "cargo-cult" rescuer from the consequences of *any* environmental degradation.)

Since it is highly improbable that the content of $\mathcal{T}$ can be expressed as an "aggregatable" homogeneous technical unit, or that this is even natural or particularly enlightening, this leaves only one mode of description that is appropriate to our purpose: the taxanomic approach— that is, a standard classification of technologies. This may appear to be a painful and puzzling exercise, especially to those who still believe in the spurious exactitude of neo-classical "technical" presumptions; but it is the only approach that can make Technos an *endogoneous* member of an empirical, heterogeneous, interactive system of economic thought . . . and takes advantage of the great wealth of literature on the history of industry and technology and its inter-relationships with political economy. Not only has a credible precedent existed for most of the 20th century in the form of the various standard industrial classifications that exist in virtually all of the world's industrialized societies (see Appendix 10), but such a system can also form the basis of a taxanomic approach for describing capital ensembles. This would address once and for all the almost irrefutable claim of Sraffa that a homogeneous technical unit of capital is an impossible construct. It also would finally honor the equally estimable, intuitive insight of Joan Robinson . . . "Capital is what capital does." The two insights are hardly unrelated, but they have not really been pursued in a practical manner, under the persistent shadow of the neo-classical syndrome. Both statements are about how the refusal to recognize the role of time in economics has led to fatal self-delusions about even the feasibility of quantification of key economic variables that are of historic and continuing import.

Towards an Empirical Framework for Classifying the Content and Structure of Technological Time
or
Accepting the Heterogeneous

$\mathcal{T}$ may be thought of as the man-made environment and topography in which economic decisions are made by individuals and institutions, and from which economic history results as a consequence of their inter-action. It may be thought of as a *"flow"* through inactive or chronologi-cal time, which may be "cut" into successive "eras," the "cuts" being determined by the particular criteria chosen as most appropriate (see Appendix 6). This "flow" attribute of $\mathfrak{T}$ also reveals its role as the most important (but not the only) changing force that causes *hysteresis*-loaded behavior in the responses (see Appendix 7) of other players in the economy (consumers, producers, retailers, financial institutions, government, etc.). The reader should refer back to the earliest pages of Chapter 1 as a "concordance" to this preceding statement. But the key point here is made explicit: Just as Technos, the "Promethean imperative," is treated as an integral, omnipresent motivation of human behavior at both the individual and institutional level—*including its irrational and aggressive aspects*—so must lags and cognitive absorption periods also be built into the economic behavior of individuals and the institutions they create for *their own purposes* (as in Telos). Hysteresis in economic behavior is no more an unnatural deviation from the perfect synchronization of response that underlies the myth of automaticity and insatiability in consumption habits than Technos is explainable as a "shock" to—or "residually" sepa-rable from—"stable" equilibrium growth paths. Human behavior is the empirical reality from which reasonable theoretical constructs are de-rived; It is not a deviant intruder to artificial constructs that must some-how be separated out as a "residual" operator. And Taxonomy is a time-honored method of dealing with otherwise unmanageable heterogeneity.

A good working classification system should capture and *link* tech-nologies that have existed in the past, those that are still economically viable and those that do not yet exist, but can be envisaged because of their obvious potential benefit, in terms of less satisfactory existing tech-nologies. Insofar as possible, the categories and classes that eventually emerge should be as self-contained as possible, but, if skillfully chosen, should reveal both the existence and the extent of *overlaps* with other classes of ostensibly disparate technologies. It is especially important to reveal why certain technologies are most important in terms of their versatility and impact, i.e., their connective and sometimes unforeseen benefits to a large number of industries and economic activities and the extent to which they can be expressed in terms of *reducing the stages of production and maintenance (or equivalents thereof) from an earlier pe-riod* (see Appendix 8). This is the closest description possible of *a true indicator of improved viability* and of a real, absolute "unit" of cost reduction, that is *not* dependent upon shifting relative costs of factor inputs. If the cost savings can be expressed in terms of *elimination* of stages of production and their constituent labor, capital forms, and inventories of materials, then it makes no difference how they are valued, how they are defined, or what the competing need for them is in other sectors of the economy. And no conceivable future cost environment can restore to economic *viability* the preceding ensemble of techniques that comprised the earlier technology which produced the relevant goods or services. For want of a better label, this class of Technos could be termed "ideal technologies." Rough examples of them may be *incompletely* and very *imperfectly* listed as follows. (It will become obvious just how indispensable a detailed and comprehensive grasp of the technological and commercial history of individual industries and economic sectors really is . . . and the critical value of contributions from specialized experts who know them best.)

As with the preceding text, the subsequent material on a proposed taxonomy of technologies should be considered as *catalytic*, inchoate, and tentative. But it is at least a beginning step out from under the dead load of the neo-classical paradigm.

- controlled heat source . . . e.g., fire (Prometheus)
- the wheel
- double entry book-keeping
- phonetic alphabets
- real number systems and the concept of zero
- paper/papyrus
- the navigator's sextant
- smelting and refining of metals, development of non-metallic synthetic materials
- agriculture and animal husbandry
- non-muscle power sources, e.g., steam engines (external combustion)
- internal combustion engines (gasoline, diesel, gas turbos, etc.)
- electric power sources and associated machinery, illumination products
- the electronic valve (vacuum tube), transistors, Linear Integrated circuits . . . "chips"
- photographic optical technology . . . motion pictures, television and video systems

- calculating, counting, and computing machines from the abacus to Babbage's calculating engine to Burroughs (Model 1914) to Bletchley Park's Colossus . . . to IBM mainframes to personal computing products . . .
- communications technology, from sunlight-on-mirror signaling systems to telegraph/Morse systems, telephone . . . wireless broadcasting and (Radar) receiving . . . high fidelity sound recording and transmission . . .
- medical antisepsis (but not surgery)
- controlled flight
- municipal water and sewage/sanitation systems
- capital flow and commercial transaction systems
- inventory control and management systems

. . . et al.

It is worth noting that a very large and historically important group of technologies are not present on the preceding list of "ideal" technologies. An *incomplete* list is as follows:

- the cotton gin
- weaving and spinning of textiles from plant and animal sources
- invention of punch-cards for the Jacquard Loom
- surgery
- woodworking and lumbering
- guns and firearms group of technologies, earlier projectile weaponry
- containerization and packaging (from clay pottery to plastics and sophisticated metal alloys and ceramics)
- shipbuilding and fabrication of water-craft, coach-work on land vehicles . . . etc., etc.

The technologies listed above do not appear on the list of "IDEAL" technologies, not because of some arbitrary and nebulous division into "High" and (presumably there ought to be) "Low" technology (see Appendix 9). Indeed, they occupy a time-honored and vital place in the ongoing history of Technos (The Promethean Imperative). But a more accurate description of their development would be: *Artisan-Incremental technologies.*

Suggested criteria for distinguishing them from "Ideal" technologies might be:

1. They are less affected by advances in basic science than "Ideal" technologies, and more driven by a gradual accumulation of "trade secrets," refinement of technique, and adaptive modification. But this is simply a generalization, that can be subjected to examination by mining the rich literature of technological and commercial history.
2. They are more acted *upon* by Ideal technologies than acting on them.
3. Their connective impact on other industries is discernibly less than those technologies which are consigned to the "Ideal" group. That is, they are more self-contained in their cognitive history than those in the Ideal group. Consequently, even if it were possible to represent the cognitive history of a technology by the isoquants shown in 3.1 and 3.2, Artisan-Incremental technologies would more closely resemble Figure 3.1 than 3.2.

Since the time of Roger Bacon (13th Century), predicting the "shape of things to come" (H.G. Wells' phrase) has been a very eternal theme of both popular and utopian/anti-utopian literature and dozens of heavily funded "think tanks." Not all of it may be described as science-*fiction*, but more often than not, the material predicted has revealed more about its authors and the mood of their times than how "things" actually "shaped" out. Some of the more "analytic" practitioners of this (Artisan-incremental, no doubt) genre, such as Jules Verne, Herman Kahn's Hudson Institute, the Rand Institute, et al, attempted to inject a more time-path irreversible direction into their efforts by predicting future technologies and their science basis, as a continuation of current trends, or a "filling in" of what they considered to be obvious *gaps* in the sequence of technological events. This procedure bore more than a little resemblance to the following obvious precedents:

1. Chemists in the 19th and 20th century filling gaps in the periodic classification of the elements with the properties of yet to be discovered elements.

2. Anthropologists and Paleontologists filling in "missing links" about the evolutionary history of Humans and other species on the basis of fossil discoveries, and "the record of the rocks."
3. Physicists at the end of the 19th century predicting the properties of yet-to-be-discovered wave bands, by filling in gaps on the electro-magnetic spectrum of light.

When applied to the affairs of Humankind (politics, economics, sociology), this type of thinking was condemned as "prophecy on the cheap. . . predicting the future as a mere continuation of the thing that is now happening . . ." (—George Orwell, who nevertheless tried it out himself . . . 1984).

With this genre in mind, as a somewhat tarnished precedent, it is not without practical purpose to go through a similar exercise of visualizing "black box" technologies and attempting to place them in a *very* early and tentative taxonomy. They are termed "black box" for now, because they can only be conceived of in terms of that they ought to do (their economic Telos, so to speak) rather than their precise internal design and the scientific basis of it. Several historical black box technologies (i.e., not in the future but a teleological past) are included.

Black Box Technology	Economic Telos	Direction of Cost Savings in Terms of Eliminated Stages of Production	Ideal Tech?	Artisan-Incremental?
"Super-Conductive" Material	Enables the delivery to consumers of a much higher percentage of produced electric power.	Reduces the need for fixed capital in the form of Hydro dams, Nuclear and Fossil-fuel-fired generating plants and associated construction and maintenance.	Yes?	
Proximity fuses (World War II ordinance innovation)	Enabled the destruction of a much higher percentage of targets because direct hits not required to trigger warhead.	Massive reduction in both the fixed capital of War (artillery) and consumable inventory (i.e., projectiles) and associated transportation and maintenance, in a war Telos. (Ships, land transport and trained military labor, i.e., human capital investment	Did incorporate basic science principles in the form of miniaturized radio transmission and receiving signals echoed from target.	Yes (confined to a war Telos—no versatility outside it.

Black Box Technology	Economic Telos	Direction of Cost Savings in Terms of Eliminated Stages of Production	Ideal Tech?	Artisan-Incremental?
Compact, inexpensive holographic imaging technology (producing transmitting, receiving) everything in realistic 3-D representation, without screens	Would create a totally superior high definition range of consumer products and processes used to produce other goods and services as well as being consumer goods in themselves, depending on acceptance into Category 2 of the CCSL.*	Would eliminate a wide range of consumer goods (TV-based) and design services that are confined to essentially flat surface imaging or 3-D modeling generated from 2-D imaging or software that creates the impression of 3-D by manipulation in 2-D. A large number of products based on 2-D imaging technology, no matter how sophisticated, would shift into Category 3 of the CCSL.	x	Yes, but debatable.

*Even from this very limited and tentative taxonomy, the entwined, complex linkages between end products and the products and processes that are constituents of their stages of production are evident. Is it a matter of "producing commodities by means of commodities" or producing commodities and developing technologies by means of common circulating technologies (and techniques)?

Black Box Technology	Economic Telos	Direction of Cost Savings in Terms of Eliminated Stages of Production	Ideal Tech?	Artisan-Incremental?
Colonoscopy —electronically-based medical technology that enables the detection, imaging, and removal of high-risk growths, along the entire relevant length of the intestinal tract, in one stage.	Contribution to maintaining and prolonging the quality of "human capital"	Eliminates three-stage procedure of Sigmoidiscope for lower end of tract, Barium detection for higher end, and often separate stage of surgical removal.	X	Yes
Controllable Fusion-based energy supply packages, mobile and stationary, with easy maintenance characteristics. (Note the avoidance of the term "Cold Fusion")	Would vastly reduce dependence on virtually all power plants based on fossil fuels, regardless of Telos of individual products.	A chain of elimination of stages of production and complementary inventory (especially in the energy group of industries) that is almost incalculable, and many entire occupations associated with them.	Yes, the most potent one conceivable.	

Black Box Technology	Economic Telos	Direction of Cost Savings in Terms of Eliminated Stages of Production	Ideal Tech?	Artisan-Incremental?
Light (Photonic) transmission of audio-visual information (i.e., micro-mirrors) switching —exclusively	Entertainment data processing and transmission for any need, business, industrial, scientific or domestic	Would eliminate the need for converting the light (photonic) signals to electronic ones and back again and all labor, material, and capital content associated with this stage of production	x	Yes
Publicly available (fully integrated) communications infrastructure (wire, satellite, fibre optic, high powered [low leakage] transmission capabilities over long distances, et al)	Anybody, anywhere can become their own multi-media "stations" for any purpose they choose. In effect "atomizes" the highly vulnerable "grand-grid" networks. Would probably result in "do it yourself" broadcasting on a much greater scale—especially by "consumers" willing to spend more on this "entertainment-educational" element of the current conception of the standard of life.	Eliminates or greatly dilutes the exclusivity of access to markets enjoyed by the great national and global networks, fixed capital infrastructures for mass communications capability.	x	Yes

Black Box Technology	Economic Telos	Direction of Cost Savings in Terms of Eliminated Stages of Production	Ideal Tech?	Artisan-Incremental?
Refrigeration	Preservation of food and pharmaceutical products, etc.	A long monograph could be written on this interaction alone! (See Diagram below)	Yes!	x

19th Century Development of canning industry and age-old technology of preservation by salting and pickling spices

"Preserves"—fresh fruit or vegetables eaten in season or stored in root cellars or in sealed jars

Refrigeration

Refrigeration combined with rapid transportation technologies makes consumption of fresh food far more available for changing tastes, i.e., Categories 1 and 2 of the CCSL.

Impact on spice trade as ancient method of preservation

Overlap

Black Box Technology	Economic Telos	Direction of Cost Savings in Terms of Eliminated Stages of Production	Ideal Tech?	Artisan-Incremental?
Distributing electric power to consumers (AC vs. DC) Westinghouse and TESLA vs. Edison, late 19th Century	Heat, light, and enabled a proliferation of appliances into Categories 1 and 2 (the "intake" part of the CCSL) that continue to this day.	AC superior in every way because it (1) reduced the "quantity" of capital goods and labor required compared to DC generation and (2) it hugely reduced the need for local power stations (especially in urban areas) and greatly reduced power losses in long distances transmission.	x	Yes

The readers can add to this list of visualized "black box" technologies to an extent limited only by their own knowledge and imagination. But a number of principles have already been captured from even this most tentative beginning:

1. When the role of time in economics is reinstated, instead of being relegated to dead clock time between "equilibrium" states, then a taxonomic approach will reveal a myriad of *cognitive and teleological* linkages through time that are *not* discontinuous and render meaningless such pseudo-temporal jargon as "long run vs. short run." After all, there is no *accurate* way of simply proclaiming the exact time when the accumulated consequences of behavior rooted in the Promethean imperative will "hit in," so to speak, and therefore no intrinsic reason why Technos should *automatically* be consigned to the "long run" except by a mode of thought which has consigned *active* time itself to the role of an exogenous shock. To paraphrase J.M. Keynes: We can all be dead in the "short run" too. . . . . It depends upon *what* "hits in," on its tim*ing*—not the time. "Timing" implies Telos; "time" (active, as in ʓ) implies Technos.

2. It is possible with a well-thought-out classification system and an expansion into *more* judiciously chosen categories (but *no more* than necessary) to demonstrate underlying, but operational linkages between ostensibly disparate technologies. For example, a practical, operational taxonomy should reveal a working connection between the tactical usage of fixed Radar installations (twin transmission and receiving towers) during the Battle of Britain (1940) (electronic-ideal technology), and the "just in time" inventory technique, part of the "ideal" technology class of inventory management/ materials handling.

In this case the linkage lies in the direction of cost savings in working capital and consumable inventory, i.e., pinpoint identification of the location, course, and number of incoming enemy aircraft obviated the need for large numbers of fighters and expensively trained aircrew to always be on standing patrol. Instead, a much smaller quantity of the working capital of a war Telos could achieve decisive strategic results through pinpoint interception at minimized distance to targets and lead times before engagement. This combination of Radar technology and (tactical) organizational technique is the equivalent of the "just in time" inventory technique of materials handling and management (for example, in standard usage for the manufacture and assembly of complex consumer durables such as motor vehicles and appliances, the retail industry, and in hospital administration, with its huge and complex needs for a large variety of inventories and maintenance services). All of these advantages over earlier techniques can be easily expressed in terms of equivalents to reducing the "stages of production," regardless of how they are delineated, defined or valued (see Appendix 11). Only the teleologies that are the *causes* of comparable economic activity are different: War is in *Sector* 2 of omega; retailing and manufacturing of consumer durables relate to *Categories* 1 and 2 of the CCSL; moralizing about the comparative values of the two Teloses is beside the point. Both are immediate and obvious causes of economic activity, regardless of such posturing (à la Scitovsky, see Appendix 2, Chapter 2) and can be described with the traditional economic and accounting terminology. It is worthy of note that the basic policy decisions (Sector 1 of omega) that led to the creation of the "chain" of radar towers along the east coast of Great Britain were taken in 1935-1936. Was the four-year lead time to their first usage ("hit in") a case of the "long run" or the "short run"? Or is it simply a case of technological time interacting with teleological timing?

The reader should apply this approach to as many connections that (s)he is familiar with in the history of technology, commerce, and industry. A suggested example is the economic impact on the capital-output ratio, of widespread usage of inexpensive personal (and portable) computers. The particular form of (fixed) capital is commercial real estate in the form of office towers and lower density storage and retail (built) space. Could the consequent reduction in this particular form of the capital-output ratio be so drastic that it approaches a potential annihilation of value as embodied in this particular *class* of capital? Is this a case of the Shivic (after the Hindu deity Shiva) principle described by Schumpeter as "creative destruction"? Or is it a somewhat weaker example that could be described as the power of transcendent ($\mathfrak{T}$) time—the Kalic principle (after the Hindu goddess Kali)?

Another example is the enormous and revolutionary benefit of antisepsis in Medicine, especially in reducing the risks of infection during surgery and convalescence. Prior to antisepsis, even the most expertly performed and artisan-perfect surgery could be easily undone by the most easily acquired and initially minor infections. All the skilled, time-consuming input of the surgery stage of treatment became futile, costly, additional stages of production. After the introduction and development of antisepsis, even the effects of hastily or ill-performed surgery were not necessarily fatal or even permanently disabling (reducing amputations) and a greater success rate could be obtained with the same number of surgeons. Any competent history of the subject has a wealth of comparative statistics—especially those dealing with military medicine during the American Civil War compared with the corresponding survival rates during the two World Wars of the twentieth century.

The whole field of medical services and related commodities and capitals would be an especially challenging classification task. Interestingly, it fits rather neatly into the overlap of Categories 1 and 2 of the CCSL (see Appendix 1 of Chapter 2, horizontally hatched area common to Categories 1 and 2). Indeed, it may be one of the few examples of the consumption accumulation process keeping up (almost in phase) with the relevant "flow" of $\mathcal{T}$.

A well-developed classification system should capture the sense of flow inherent in $\mathcal{T}$. This is tantamount to emphasizing the *continuity* of the cognitive element in technological progress rather than engaging in a continuing campaign of separating, dichotomizing, and dis-aggregating its myriad and heterogeneous interconnections. This leads almost naturally toward a taxonomy that emphasizes and identifies degrees of *overlap* and *co-existence* of techniques and technologies, rather than assigning spurious quantification and homogeneity to that which has been questionably dis-aggregated and not sufficiently defined for such operations in the first place.

Following are several examples of overlap in time and co-existence of techniques and technologies that a working taxonomy should accommodate.

1. *Automobile transmissions*: Automatic transmissions constitute the majority of transmissions on passenger automobiles. But they *co-exist* with manual transmissions on most heavy cargo-hauling commercial vehicles which operate in a much different but co-existing cost environment. However, in technological time, earlier "half-way house" versions of auto-

matic transmissions such as hydra-matic and fluid drive over-
lapped with the more or less fully developed version of automatic transmission *technique*.

2. *Harvesters, reapers, threshers*: The McCormick reaper's
    blade configuration continues to be the dominant one in agri
    culture for harvesting grain crops. For decades they contin-
    ued to be "towed" by draught horses which were themselves
    the product of centuries of highly developed (artisan-incre-
    mental) breeding techniques and orally transmitted knowl-
    edge. They still represented a clear eliminator of the labor-
    intensive sickle-swinging stage of production, in any
    conceivable cost environment *until* the development of steam
    and subsequently internal combustion powered tractors.
    Draught horses as muscle-powered tractors are still economi-
    cally viable in some small- to medium-scale agricultural cost
    environments (co-existence). But they have virtually no vi-
    ability for any economies of scale as long as cheap fossil fuel
    does not vanish from the planet.

3. Jet-powered commercial air transport continues to co-exist
    with propellor-based air transport. The number of different
    cost environments in the air transportation industries is so
    great that it is impossible to envisage a future cost environ-
    ment that does not leave room for at least a few propellor-
    based models. Indeed, the incredibly viable DC-3, in slowly
    declining numbers, has co-existed for decades with far more
    sophisticated (?) aviation technologies.

4. During the early years of "talkies" in the motion picture
    industry the dominant technology was the "Vita-Phone" sys-
    tem . . . essentially a gigantic record disc (electro-mechani-
    cal turntable) system. Because of its inability to remain in a
    perfectly balanced state in a high vibration environment, it
    always fell out of synchronization with the lip movements of
    the actors in the film strips it was supposedly accompanying.
    It required constant labor-intensive attendance, and contin-
    ued to produce unintentionally hilarious results (low quality
    service) in spite of such attention. The period of overlap was

mercifully short (several years) until it was eliminated completely (along with all its accompanying labor and hardware) by the integrated sound track (magnetic tape).

5. The container, utensils, materials, and packaging group of techniques and technologies are probably the prime example of overlap and co-existence in *time* and space. There always seems to be some cost environment that can make even the most ancient forms of packaging and containerization economically viable. Archeologists could render much assistance on this particular example of overlap and continuity in technological (cognitive) time (see Figure 3.1 again).

6. The technicolor process, first introduced into the motion picture industry in the mid-1930s, superseded the occasionally tried but commercially unviable, labor-intensive, manual methods of hand-coloring on a frame-by-frame basis. There was virtually no overlap with these earlier artisan techniques. But the technicolor process and its subsequent refinements co-existed for more than five decades with numerous successful improvements until the age of digital colorization. One of the potential benefits that would be derived from a good working classification of technologies and techniques is the development of a rigorous *economic* definition of obsolescence. Since the concept of "obsolete" (or obsolescence) embodies the notion of supersession through some form of irreversible, evolutionary time, it cannot be derived from a conceptual framework that insists on its "path-independence" from active time. It may be a productive exercise to start with the idea of a gradual loss of viability as a particular technology or technique becomes less and less frequent as a "best practice" match for those cost environments having the highest probability of occurrence (see Appendix 12).

But this approach can only work from an evolutionary historical-empirical basis, wherein the heterogeneous universe of technological and industrial history is tamed by a well developed and sophisticated taxonomy of Technos, the Promethean Imperative; that is, the compulsion to be "technical" or unnecessarily abstract would have to be suppressed.

The subject's aspirations to "predictive power" will be much better served by this acceptance of the heterogeneous and its requirement for the less glamourous skills of the classifier, the cataloguer and the corroborator. The taxanomic approach, combined with an acceptance of the dominant role of ᘔ, could clarify one notorious problem for which a feasible solution may not even exist within the time-path independent neoclassical "paradigm." Instead of asking how it is possible to separate the effects of technological advance from those of economies of scale, it may be better to ask whether there is perhaps a mutually beneficial interaction (analagous to a catalytic or symbiotic relationship) between the incentive to improve the technology of a particular industry and the prospect of an increased scale of demand. A practical test case of this scenario is Canada's Alberta tar sands, reputed to be equal in potential output to those of Saudi Arabia. Under what circumstances would it be worthwhile to anticipate such an increase in scale of demand, given the huge natural cost advantages of extracting oil from Saudi Arabia? Would they likely arise from causes that have more to do with political instability or cycles of self-destructive irrationality in mass behavior? Such an analysis would also remind us of Veblen's warning to never "isolate" economic decisions and events from the consequences of behavior rooted in other aspects of the "conscious life," or Teloses, in the language of this exposition. . . . (see Chapter 2, especially the first paragraph, as a concordance).

A Modest Proposal

In Norbert Wiener's "God and Golem" 1964, the following trenchant comment appeared which sums up the mindset of the neoclassical straitjacket.

"The success of mathematical physics led the social scientists to be jealous of its power without quite understanding the intellectual attitudes that had contributed to the power." As Wiener explains further: "The mathematical physics of 1850" (this early date may be an especially unkind cut on his part) became "the mode of the social sciences." Wiener goes on to say that "very few econometricians are aware that, if they are to *imitate* the procedure of modern physics, and not its *mere appearances* (perhaps the unkindest *cut* of all), a mathematical economics must begin with a critical account (i.e., rigorous definitions?) of these quantitative notions and the means adopted for collecting and *measuring* them." Since Wiener spent many years on the same premises as the most prominent "imitators" he must have been keenly aware of just how the problem of *defining* key economic variables to a point where they could be meaningfully manipulated as homogenous "technical" units had, in effect, defeated their best efforts to attain the "scientific" respectability that only "quantifiability" can bestow. With this perhaps definitive *limiting* principle on the subject as a subliminal guideline we can, in a humbler vein, pose the following question: Is there at least some procedure that accepts implicitly the subject's inherent limitations or, more to the point, its own unique nature by actually searching for the *boundaries* within which some degree of "quantifiability" is feasible, and beyond which this aspiration is merely spurious or being deliberately or unwittingly abused? This is the same as asking how far we can go with many of the traditional operations of economic estimation, calculation, and comparative valuation . . . or at what point do they cease to convey ordinal meaning?

An incomplete list of such operations, which are the stuff of "economic arithmetic" include indexing (choosing appropriate deflators), valuations of capital (see Appendix 14) and associated variables (e.g., the capital co-efficient or capital/output ratio), Gross Domestic Product and Aggregate Incomes, depreciation estimates (see Appendix 14), investment, savings, and associated propensities and ratios, inventory valuations, prices, costs of commodities, etc. (especially for purposes of analysis and comparison through time). In effect we are searching for some kind of protocol of criteria to place "cuts" (see appendix 15) in $\mathcal{T}$, such that there is sufficient similarity in the historical *eras between the cuts*, to permit operations that are based on assumptions of reasonable homogeneity in the variables being manipulated. In short, assumptions about the validity of such comparative "arithmetic" would be recognized as highly temporal, provisional at best. But at least some kind of number could be assigned, however roughly, to the "era" of $\mathcal{T}$ for which certain chosen operations could be performed in terms of dollars, pounds, marks, francs, rupees, sheckels, yen, etc. And hopefully, this would make the statistical mesh that attempts to capture such variables finer. But it is not realistic to expect that even a moderately successful application of the "cut" idea to an economic context would yield the crisp mathematical clarity of the analogues described in Appendix 15.

Figure 3.6

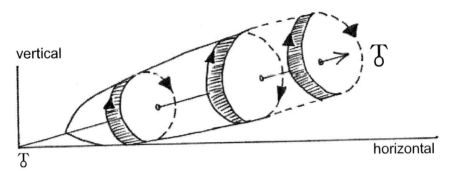

Consider Figure 3.6 above.

The arrow (vector) Ⴀ shows the direction of Technological time. Attributing magnitude to Ⴀ in this context has no economic interpretation, i.e., the fragile "quantifiability" limits of even this simple geometric illustration would already have been exaggerated. The slices of varying thickness and diameter may be interpreted as the boundaries of unique "eras" in Ⴀ with sufficient similarity, as determined by the protocol of criteria, to permit the standard operations described previously.

As they approach almost infinitely thin (membrane) thickness, they may be interpreted as the cross-sections of a "Say's law" stationary (market) economy—"snapshots" in the flow of Ⴀ, so to speak. This interpretation is consistent with the historic understanding in economic thought, that a perfect Say-Wairas market economy, one of repetitive unimpeded circular flow, is the legitimate domain of:

- perfect competition
- perfectly automatic market-clearing mechanisms
- eternal repetition of consumer wants,
- perfect synchronization of consumer responses to stimuli in the market, e.g., price changes, product knowledge,
- constant vintage capital as a real measurable, homogenous unit,
- real interest rates are zero (Schumpeter) in the absence of technical change,
- The same set of investment opportunities makes the same rounds continuously and really amounts to little more than

the replacement of physically depreciated constant vintage capital goods.

• Heuristic operations and methodologies such as Linear programming, involving fixed technical coefficients and easily identifiable and "quantifiable" factors of production, which may be considered to act conjointly in optimally allocated ensembles of land, raw materials, labor and capital, are sufficient to explain all productive activity.

• Money is a "veil" whose behavior may be treated just like any other commodity in the exchange market place. Any interesting power relationships arising from differential control of this "commodity" may be disregarded.

• Any barriers to its smooth, unimpeded circular flow may be treated as accumulations of "rigidities" or periods of adjustment easily smoothed out; there is no such thing as hysteresis or "unpredictable" gaps in the behavior of economic man or in the responses of the institutions he has created and with which he interacts.

• Any economic phenomena can be represented as perfectly predictable sequences of motion on the road to Equilibrium. Indeed, they are usually represented within this *perfectly legitimate limited domain* to have already taken place. (Hayek, *The Sensory Order* and *Economics and Knowledge*, 1937)

Returning to Figure 3.6 . . . The place and orientation of the horizontal and vertical axes does have an economic interpretation, as does the diameters of the Say's Law/circular flow slabs (Virtual markets along ♉).

1. If the axes are placed such that the horizontal (x) axis is parallel to the vector of ♉, and the circular-flow slabs are always the same diameter, then a repetitive stationary state with constant population, constant participation rate, and no business cycle is described. ♉ is constant (not the orientation shown). This case corresponds to the great Ludwig V. Mises' concept of the Evenly Rotating Economy—ERE for short—which he regarded as being simply an analytic foil rather than a model of reality . . . or an "ought to be" (Hume).

2. As shown in Figure 3.6, the flow of technological time (as gauged by its angle to the horizontal) is positive, i.e., economic history has some degree of correspondence with technological "progress" however estimated. If the population and labor participation rate are constant then there is significant growth in per capita prosperity, no matter how it is measured; in terms of this figure the pie is literally growing bigger and bigger for a constant population.

3. If the "slabs" are of constant size and the vector of Υ is similar in orientation to what is shown in 3.6, this may be interpreted as a situation where technology had to "progress" just to maintain the same level of prosperity, perhaps because of rapid population growth or depletion of natural resources, or some combination of the two.

The reader may "thought experiment" with other combinations of the given parameters. But the most important object of the exercise is to develop an acceptable protocol of criteria which determines the placement of the "cuts."

The best starting point for this task is to first develop a reasonably universal taxonomy of technologies and techniques from which such criteria might be worked out agorithmically and inductively, once a canon of taxa has been established (e.g., a cut may be placed on the basis of the presence or absence of certain combinations of ideal technologies).

It should also be evident how further development and refinement of the basic ideas and directions advocated in this chapter will erase whatever small interest may remain with the "short run" vs. "long run" issue, which could only have arisen as the untreatable effluent of a mindset, that eschewed the very idea of active time as a vital factor in economic analysis.

Is Technological Innovation a *Deus Ex Machina*?

A popular trend among some theorists in recent years has been to describe technological change as a form of "Spontaneous Generation." In this way, Technos, the Promethean Imperative, is reduced to weed-like, self-hybridizing growth (like Parthenogenesis?) as the consequence of some sort of endogenous drive that cannot stop itself from combining and permuting every untried, pre-existing technology and technique. It almost appears that these particular writers, having lost faith in the ability of the neoclassical school to sustain their mimesis of 19th century energy physics, have found another savior in the biology of the 18th century, *before Spallanzani.*

Is this kind of theorizing merely a recrudescence of dormant vitalism? New packaging for the old crackpot determinism of technocracy? Or perhaps a gross abuse of Schumpeter's ideas about the role of the entrepreneur, and development as the result of new combinations and arrangements?

To illustrate in the simplest terms what the gist of such theorizing really amounts to, consider Figure 3.7 below.

Figure 3.7

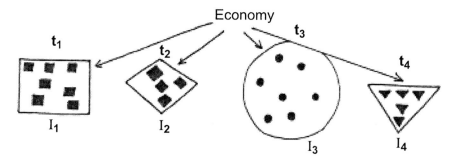

In Figure 3.7, a simple economy consists of four industries, I_1 to I_4 inclusive. Each industry consists of only one technology, t_1 to t_4 inclusive, with their own unique set of constituent techniques. Each industry produces only one commodity with its one technology. If each industry produced several commodities (related) with a separate technology for each commodity, then the set of all technologies in each industry that produced all its particular commodities to a certain standard of performance or quality could be described as "state of the art" for that industry. In this case the title is particularly easy to win because there is no competition. If there was a corresponding industry in a competing foreign jurisdiction, and comparable standards of quality, then the winner would be "state of the art" . . . like the great swordsmiths who made Samurai swords were reputed to be.

Then, according to the spontaneous breeding notion of technological growth, the number of new technologies (and techniques) can increase even better than exponentially, merely as the result of hybrid combining from previous generations of technologies. Such a view of the creative process is not very flattering to either scientific and technical innovators, nor to the basic premises of patent examiners. On this basis they would refuse virtually all applications on the grounds that they "are obvious from the prior art."

1. The techniques within a given technology may combine ("endogeneously" of course, and regardless of development costs) to form another technique within that technology.
2. The techniques within a particular technology may breed to generate another technology, i.e., another set of techniques which characterized another technology.
3. The component techniques of different technologies may hybridize to produce either new techniques in any number of them, or a new technology . . . (ad infinitum?).

The implications of—and motivations behind—this kind of thinking leave little to the imagination.

It could easily furnish a means of slipping the unobtrusive fallacy of "automatic compensation" through the back door in order to restore some form of dubious symmetry that might replace that of *Utility/Technology* as complementary "fields." After all, if spontaneous breeding of technical progress (like a "free good"?) can be complemented symmetrically by a perfectly automatic and synchronized response from the consumption accumulation process, why worry about complex, contingent ("ify") responses from the hystereses-loaded human behavior of homo-economus and the institutions that carry it? It's insatiable, perfectly synchronized in its reaction time and therefore "guarantees the 'law' of automatic compensation, without any fear of macro-economic instability of the 'structural' kind, n'est pas? In effect, this ultimate form of determinism in human behavior can now explain economic history (past, present, and future) by imposing robot-like behavior on *both* Telos and Technos." There is no complex interaction between them, no need to even consider the role of Telos and the current conception of the standard of life, and how they can create or deny economic viability to even the most ingenious act of the Promethean Imperative.

Progress itself has become "automated." If economic history itself has become perfectly predictable as the road of *automatic* progress then there is no time at all in the Bergsonian sense (durée) as referred to in

Appendix 6. All time is dead clock time between magically appearing, successive equilibrium states.

The reader should return to the economic parable in Appendix 15. Its moral becomes even clearer. There is no "flow" of technological time, and therefore no real economic history without the viability that Telos sires in its interaction with Technos. But economic history consists of those very successive, unique, virtual markets that are formed in each era of technological time. In Veblen's terms, that kind of theoretical floundering constitutes the original sin of "isolating" economic behavior from the uniquely human "conscious life."

The *Manifold* Nature of Technological Time Ꝩ
or
There's much more to it than change in the technology of producing goods and services and/or productivity.

Because of its manifold nature, technological time cannot be easily reduced to traditional time series analysis. Differences in kind, heterogeneity, interaction, emergences (Samuel Alexander's explicitly gestalt-loaded conception of how Ꝩime forms out of "point-instants," and "pure-events") are the key to developing this operational concept. Further investigation into Samuel Alexander's vision of real time reveals an *image* of Ꝩime operating on materiality (the "operand"?) as a kind of "core-boring." It should also inspire the few readers who might be interested in the philosophical "undercarriage" of Ꝩ that it could be considered a kind of "durée" (Henri Bergson—The kind of durée most appropriate for economic analysis? After all, economics requires its own distinct patterns of thought ("sui-generis"—George Shackle) especially about how it handles real time. Consequently, we shall attempt to summarize the "*furniture*" of Ꝩechnological time, in the hope that it will lead to further development of the concept via the participation of our readers.

1. Improvement in the technologies of producing and distributing the commodities and services that comprise the CCSL and Sector 2 of ω (omega) See Chapter 2. *Era of slow or rapid progress in productivity.*
2. The "cognitive" topography of particular "eras" of Ꝩechnological time. Dominant and "ideal" Technologies, tacit knowledge (Hayek), "know-how," "Alertness" of entrepreneurs,

educational levels, patterns of asymmetric knowledge (*not* "information").

3. The relative scarcity of and ease of availability of resources, and the matèriel base that would sustain the choices, the "ends" the "tastes" that characterize the "culture of consumption" during particular eras. (Minerals, choice of foods, transportation, clothing etc.)

4. Attitudes toward the opportunity costs incurred by choosing particular production technologies to produce our chosen lifestyles and further societal "goals" (Sector 2 of Omega). Some societies would choose almost fatal despoilation of the physical and social environments to achieve their "ends" . . . whether hedonistic (CCSL) or political and ideological.

5. The "institutional" topography of particular societies and how they facilitate changes in attitudes toward risk, mediating uncertainty, debt-tolerance, terms of trade, distribution of wealth, taxation, class structure, market-cultures etc. (i.e., cultures of frugality, caution and restraint, cultures of "conspicuous conception"). In this respect we should recall the "parable" of Napoleon's mother. Napoleon wrote to her and asked her why she did not spend the remittances he sent to her on an appropriately "regal" life-style, as befitted the mother of a great emperor (and his Prince, Princesses siblings). She replied "we will have need of it, when all this is over"

$$\underset{\substack{\text{ascetic frugality}\\ \infty}}{\text{Savonarola}} \xleftarrow{\text{tends}} \theta \xrightarrow{\text{tends}} \underset{\text{insatiability}}{\text{McCulloch's Law?}}$$

Return to Chapter 2 to understand this.

6. The dominant commodity composition (the CCSL) and products and services associated with Sector 2 of ω (Omega). It is this particular "furniture" of 𝔗echnological Time where the Gestalt Principles Operation is most conspicuous, and where The "Imputation Principle of Friedrich Von Wieser becomes an "aid to navigation" in understanding how the Telos $\longleftrightarrow$ 𝔗echnos nexus functions.

A factor of production (e.g., labor, specialized skills, and equipment) can be rendered obsolescent or even "collapsed" to value-zero, in one of two ways.

1. It can be part of a stage of production that is "superceded" by an authentic improvement in the technology of production. But the particular commodity of service (whether part of the CCSL or Sector 2) still remains as part of the "topography" of economic activity.

Economic Obsolescence—Its True Meaning?

2. The distinct elements of the CCSL or the aspects of Sector 2 with which these factors of production are associated, passes out of the CCSL and/or Sector 2. In "Austrian" terms, the "ends" of these particular "means" vanished. (See quote from Eugen Von Bohm Bawerk on Title Page) *and* see Chapter 5 for an example from Sector 2—the collapse of value for militarily skilled labor, when demobilization hit in-in 1945. In other words, these particular factors of production took their value in the market from the Telos to which they were contributing; when the Telos vanished, their value vanished, with their *raison d'être*. This is really an illustration of the intensely gestalt nature of The Imputation Principle: "It is this tendency to derive the meaning (value), the sense of individualities (from the whole, not the summation of individualities to the whole)"—which contributes "to the advancement in other fields (apart from Physics)—even moreso than in Physics."—Otto Neurath in a letter to Ernst Mach, circa 1915. A good explanation of Telos leading Technos or "Gestalt-Drag" or Henri Bergson's "actualization from the virtual (whole) into the heterogeneous"—processes that are always linked to purposeful actions . . . and do not necessarily lead to even momentary states of "equilibrium."

Unfortunately in 1945 poor Otto met a bad "end" so to speak; not only was he a hardcore Marxist advocate of abolishing any and all manifestations of free-market activity. He also was on the "losing end" of the "Socialist calculation debate"—a firm believer in the omniscient powers of planning what is best for everybody down to the last detail. But his (rare?) lapse into sanity, quoted above, was a reversal of "vector" of his mentor's version of the "Labor Theory of Value." Just as the idea of consumers freely choosing the goods and services they want, according to their own value-loadings. (See Chapter 2, θ, The Threshold of Consumption, CCSL, et al.) It is at odds with Marx's bizarre rant about "commodity fetishism." He obviously hated the very notion of consumer sovereignty—The "ends"—the Teloses that give labor value for services performed; just as the great Friedrich Von Wieser clearly understood.

Appendix 1

Differences between societies in their experiences of the flow of technological time have often given rise to such euphemisms as "under-developed" . . . "developing" . . . "behind the times" . . . "in a time warp" . . . "frozen in time" . . . and more candidly, "backward." Such gaps in technological time have often proved to be an irresistible temptation to successful aggression and domination by the nation whose economy is further ahead in technological time. Yet, the "winner" and the "loser" are living in the same chronological time and the winner often has far less population and natural resources. This is a case where popular parlance has grasped instinctively what some of the "learned" have never quite understood.

Appendix 2

It should be emphasized that it is *not asserted* here that substitution is *always* congruent with authentic improvements in the technologies of production—only that substitution is a valid and obvious form of it. The simplest illustration of this point is in the polar extreme of military behavior. Improvements in the fighting efficiency of one army compared to another can almost always be effected by increasing the quantity and associated investment in training of *known* forms of military capital, e.g., tanks, missiles, aircraft, medical corps. Similar superiority can also be gained by the introduction of *new* weaponry and technology by one side. The difference between the two is often more obvious in a military scenario than in an economy driven mainly by the CCSL. But mixtures of the two are commonplace in a military setting as well; it is simply another example of the cognitive linkage between different states of technology. This reality is better described by further development of the idea of technological time, rather than an insistence on the false dichotomy of "substitution vs. technological innovation" which arises naturally from the strait jacket of the equilibrium cum field metaphor of the neoclassical paradigm. This application, i.e., an "event-cut" that resolves this century-old polemic cannot be fully developed all in "one gulp" so to speak. But it can at least be opened up for *or* by our readers.

In this early development of resolving "substitution vs. improvement in productive technology," we shall attempt to demonstrate as consistently as possible the connections between this "false problem" as defined by Henri Bergson, *and . . .*

1. The principle of obsolescence, which is untreatable by the "timeless" neoclassical paradigm; but is vital to explaining the changing needs for "quantity of work" needed at a particular point in Technological time and its relationship to our criterion of an "unambiguous elimination of a stage of production—or equivalence," and its *practical* implications for labor and immigration policy development.

2. The development of criteria for determining the placement of the "cut" in the spirit of "the events are the Time" *and* order of events counts, i.e., the "cut" *is* the superceding point in differentiating one "kind" of (local, industry-specific). Technological Time from the preceding one, in a par-

ticular production process in a specified sector, as identified by the SIC (Standard Industrial Classification) codes—which are highly developed for use in Economic Statistics and Taxation/Regulatory agencies.

3. It is absolutely necessary to provide a qualitative description of the "superceding" event that appears on our industrial— (learning) history real (events are the) time "isoquant." The reader should keep in mind that we are trying to preserve (or at least salvage) as much of this geometrical representation as possible, despite the deep dissatisfaction with what it really represents—expressed in the early text of Chapter 3. In short, apply case histories from the history of specific industries.

Consider the following "modified" learning-curve-isoquant representation of change, as a sequence of events that *are* the flow of Technological Time in a particular industry, characterized by the commodities it produces . . . and which have a definable "mapping" in Categories 1 and/or 2 of the CCSL (Current Conception of the Standard of Life). See Chapter 2.

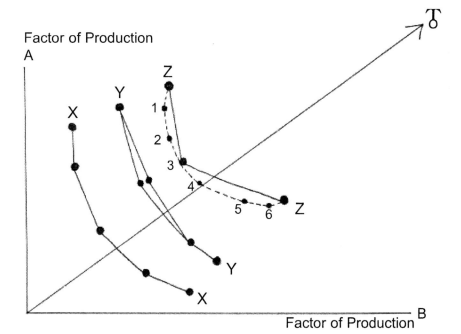

$x - x$ isoquant has five "techniques" which represent the "state" of productive technology in that industry at that "point" in its technological history.

At $y - y$ the "state" of productive technology has been "winnowed" to four techniques.

At $z - z$ the state of productive technology has been "winnowed" to three techniques. But we have added in six more "lesser" points which appear to "smooth out" the learning curve, *without* eliminating any more techniques. We could have filled in corresponding "smoothers" on $x - x$ and $y - y$ corresponding to the economic variables of their Technological Times. What the points "represent" are "substitution" events, which may be described as "tacit" knowledge (Hayek), local "know-how," "alertness" applied on the spot, to confront the ebb and flow of daily economic life, e.g., changes in the relative costs of materièl inventory; changes in supplier sources, shifts in transaction costs, variations in systems design, changes the relative availability of different kinds of labor and vital materièl. But the main principle to be grasped is this: A true substitution event doesn't eliminate any of the techniques that constituted the previous "state of the art" of the productive technology. It cannot be described by "pecuniary" (one of Veblen's favorite epithets) quantity—hence the need for accompanying qualitative description. As an industry becomes "mature" this particular representation would tend to stall at the $z - z$ isoquant. Perhaps more "smoothers" would cluster between the 3 points, perhaps not. But where the key points actually change in number (+ or -) we have a "cut" in the Technological time of the industry's productive technology that supercedes the previous state, i.e., the previous "state" has in some way been rendered "obsolescent." Arguably, true substitution takes place *within* techniques, i.e., it may be called an expansion of the "substitution"—matrix to maturity.

However, there are, by way of example, cases where what would be described as "substitution" colloquially are actually significant changes in the industry's Technological Time, e.g., the discovery of a wide array of heat-resistant materièls and alloys greatly reduced the need (and weight) for complicated cooling apparatus such as fans, vanes, etc., i.e., they "superceded" unnecessary complexity and weight. *Case for investigation*: The interested reader should consult the various accounts of the early years of jet engine manufacturing. For example, when Germany was cut off by the allied embargo from her supply of heat-resistant metals, the designers of the Messerschmidt 262 had to "substitute" the weighty, component-loaded cooling designs, which the "discovery" of heat-resistant alloys had superceded. Similarly, the development of heat engines as the primary motive power for sea-going vessels was no mere "substitution" of "steam for sail." It virtually wiped out all the paraphernalia, labor-skills, kinds of capital and much of the materièl associated with thousands of years of "The Age of Sail."

One interesting and by no means "hypothetical" application of this approach, with definite policy implications is described below and should be kept in mind when we come to Chapter 6—The extension of Friedrich Von Wieser's idea of opportunity costs (foregone benefits of making particular choices):

Consider a productive technology (existing "best practice" in terms of direct and immediate cost) but clearly threatening to lead to a scenario that we have called "the passenger pigeon scenario" or the "tragedy of the commons" or unacceptable "collateral damage" to our physical or social environment—resource exhaustion is the most obvious and unambiguous spectre.

But the commodities that *impute* value to all these input factors of production remain solidly entrenched in Categories 1 and 2 of the CCSL. Note that Von Wieser's principle of the imputation of factor value, *back* from their exchange value in the market (an intensely gestalt-loaded concept of value indeed) virtually cries out for recognition here. Then, the "unchoosing" of the "best practice" technology could lead to a less "efficient" one by straightforward "least cost" criteria—perhaps even a "superceded" one. Or even to the "substitution" of more immediately costly synthetic materials, or even more labor-intensive techniques/technologies. (See the case histories of the "high-tech" fishing industry and mega-output automobile production in Chapter 6)—i.e., wood substitutes are notoriously expensive compared to the "easy" availability of the natural material—*for now*. These may well constitute "best-practice" technologies in terms of opportunity costs, but not direct costs of production. Some of them are pure substitution; others are substitution as technical advance for "conservation's sake." It should also be recalled that Von Wieser was the least laissee-faire-inclined of all the "Austrians" and had the greatest dread of social instability and the "free markets" potential for contributing to it.

It is left to the reader's judgment whether or not the preceding resolution of this century-old dilemma is "perfect" . . . or whether the old isoquant representation of productive technology has reached its "outer limits." But we are confident that the preceding exposition finally introduces a "new beginning" that will organize the vast array of industrial and Technological history toward some definitive policy applications, and provides a "good-fit" for "taming" all this "raw" information toward meaningful explanation. It is also obvious why this subject cannot be "aggregated" or "quantified" toward some *meaningful end*, in the sense that Menger, Von Wieser, Hayek, Mises, et al would have understood.

Appendix 3

After 1960 it became a commonplace observation to note that both Germany and Japan had been done an economic favor by the strategic bombing of World War II. This had resulted in the annihilation of capital value in the literal sense of the term, i.e., since a huge percentage of their fixed capital goods and equipment (regardless of vintage) had been subjected to the ultimate form of Schumpeter's "creative destruction," both nations had no other choice but to start over with the very latest in "state of the art" capital goods and productive technology. The accuracy of such observations has yet to be confirmed, but the underlying inference that superior productive technology is largely embodied in newer vintages of "machinery" (classical economists' term) and equipment is obvious. This would not seem to allow much room for the contributions of accumulated "human capital"—One more reason for the necessity of a gestalt, "black box" concept like ϑ.

Appendix 4

Another equally lethal expression of blind faith is the complementary doctrine of automatic compensation and its *underlying* dogma of consumer insatiability. There have been sightings as recently as 1996, e.g., "Virtually *underlying all* economists' contributions to the debates was a fundamental optimism about the ability of the economy to re-absorb labor." (—*Technological Unemployment and Structural Unemployment Debates*, page 2075, by Gregory R. Woiral, London, Greenwood Press, 1996.) The reader should also re-examine Figure 2.1 of Chapter 2, and the accompanying text, which is directly related to this point.

Appendix 5

Indeed, the need for the concept of ϑ may well have been engendered by the inherent impossibility of ever "quantifying" such key economic concepts as capital, separation of technological innovation from the contribution to productivity of capital accumulation, total factor productivity, substitution vs. technical improvement, unemployment, etc. It should be emphasized that an inability to quantify key economic variables to the standards of 19th century energy physics does not detract in any way from their operational reality or their vital role in economic thought.

Appendix 6

If the reader is so inclined (s)he may compare $\mathcal{T}$ to the concept of "duration/durée" of the philosopher Henri Bergson. Bergson developed the concept of durée *in contrast to* the concept of quantitative or chronological time. One of the key attributes of durée is that it must constitute a time magnitude, without being accessible to a purely quantitative representation.

Appendix 7

The reader should refer back to page 30 of Chapter Two, as a concordance with one of Veblen's primary ideas about adaptation to technical change as a determinant of economic history.

Appendix 8

This criterion should be compared to the notion of "compressing" the average "period of production" of the industry, as defined by the Austrian school of capital theory. As a useful concordance with this appendix, the reader should consult the earlier section of this chapter dealing with what an advance in the technology of production allows to happen. ("Compression of the quantity of work required. . .")

Appendix 9

The reader should refer back to the earlier part of the chapter as a concordance in which it is stated that "a logical consequence of an operational description of technological change ought to be . . . a subsuming of vague and confusing dichotomies such as . . . 'high' . . . and 'low' technology. . ." Perhaps this example is an early case of how the taxonomic approach can wield "Occam's Razor" in ridding the world of at least one meaningless cliché.

Appendix 10

Taxonomic thinking is an indispensable and ingeniously applied building block of Vasily Leontieff's Input-Output matrices, a worthy descendant of a traditional thought-tool first initiated in Qusnay's *Tableau Economique* (1759).

Appendix 11

The reader should refer back to Figure 3.2 and the text following it. The *reduced stages of production criterion* for defining an indisputable improvement in technology and economic *viability* is a veritable Gordion knot solution when compared with anything that could be possibly inferred from Figure 3.2, i.e., the criterion for an improvement in productive technology is quite rigorous; the best practice technique of $\mathcal{T}_2$ must yield lower costs than the best practice technique of $\mathcal{T}_1$ which requires that the more contemporary technology (as represented by the isoquant $\mathcal{T}_2 - \mathcal{T}_2$) must not only be sufficiently flexible to reduce the optimal costs associated with the *same* cost array of factor inputs—it must also reduce them from the optimal costs of $\mathcal{T}_1$ even if a more malleable cost environment prevailed during $\mathcal{T}_1$. This is a very revealing commentary on the limitations of the field metaphor's capability (as represented by isoquants) for dealing with events in active, evolutionary time; even when squeezed to unrealistic limits. Precisely because it presumes to be independent of the trajectory of evolutionary time, it fails to capture that $\mathcal{T}$ changes the "universe" of economic viability.

Appendix 12

A Parable of Floundering Technos or the Viability That Never Was

In his autobiography *Arrow in the Blue* (Macmillan Company, New York, 1961, pages 14 and 15), Arthur Koestler describes a demonstration of a "stupendous invention" that he witnessed as a child in Budapest just before the outbreak of World War I. " A truck drawn by six horses rumbled into the courtyard . . . and half a dozen men, sweating and groaning, carried a monstrous machine up the stairs into our smoking room." Koestler goes on to describe "an electrical contraption . . . with wires, wheels and levers . . . in its belly, which emitted an occasional frightening spark and . . . in the end there came a big flash, accompanied by the smell of burnt rubber and the shrieks of the cook and maid . . . darkness descended over the flat. . ."

After an hour or so the thing really started to work. It rumbled and clattered like an old fashioned printing press and its huge body, which occupied half the length of a wall, trembled so violently that all the ash trays, bronze nymphs and cuspidors . . . danced on their bases". . . and what was the economic Telos of this "monstrous machine"? Koestler's father was handed a "bundle of tattered envelopes of various sizes. . . . He pushed the sealed envelopes, *one by one* into a slot in the machine while Professor Nathan standing on tiptoe at the other end extracted from a second slot the same envelopes . . . which had entered the machine sealed and were now cut open."

"'But what is it for?' Asked my mother. . . ."

Older readers will recall that this not unusual twist in the Promethean Imperative became, in the hands of a great master of ironic humor, the cartoonist/artist Rube Goldberg, a unique genre in its own right. The source of the humor was, of course, the irrelevance of the "stupendous" invention to any conceivable Telos of "economic man."

Appendix 13

One obvious illustration of this point occurred during the deadly "one-upsmanship" duels of technology and organizational technique that characterized the Battle of the Atlantic during the Second World War. It was discovered that obsolescent (for combat) aircraft and reconnaissance aircraft of conventional vintage (operands?) could be fitted with the now abundantly produced, inexpensive, compact, and highly portable Radar sets ("operators"?). This organizational configuration caused a striking *rise* ("transformation") in both the detection and (through co-ordination with escort vessels) targeting and destruction of U-Boats, as well as in successful deliveries of cargoes to their destinations. In terms of the criteria for classifying technologies tentatively begun in this chapter as an antidote to the sterile dead-end of the neoclassical field metaphor, this constitutes an unambiguous *chain* of decrease in the stages of production, accompanied by an unambiguous rise in productivity (no matter how it is measured) with less of the quantity, volume, and bulk of the capital goods and various inventories of a war Telos. It would not be difficult to find hundreds of examples of this class of technological progress in other categories of the CCSL. Indeed, this phenomenon might qualify as a separate class of technologies, based on their powers of *retro-fit* and ease of *modification*, to existing factors of production, to achieve higher productivity with a *net* decrease in the bulk and volume of such factors. Where does this leave theories of "embodiment" and the technical bias of capital?

Appendix 14

If there really existed such constructs as quantifiable, homogeneous, technical units of capital whose value was independent of the rate of interest and profit as neoclassical theory actually requires, then accountants' depreciation conventions would converge to the "straight line" method . . . and "constant vintage capital" would be a reality as well as a consequence of the same circular thinking within which the field metaphor and the equilibrium paradigm flourish.

Appendix 15

The idea of a "cut" calls to mind the analogue of a Dedekind *cut* in Mathematics, an ingenious but simple criteria used to divide real numbers into rational and irrational numbers. Another example of this approach in a quite different context is the Chaitin-Kolmogorov "cut" used to differentiate "strings" generated by computer programs into "simple" and "complex," i.e., "a given string is simple if the string may be generated by a computer program that is significantly shorter than the string itself. Otherwise it is complex." (In this context a computer program is itself a "string" of symbols . . . in the form of binary sequences—strings of 0's and 1's.)

In a more laconic but Poetic way we should consider:

In a moment
You see something pass,
From past to future,
Uncut by the knives of time!

—Vladimir Mayakovsky, 1894 - 1930
Russian Futurist poet

Appendix 16

Arguably, the neoclassical insistence that substitution along a given production function (in the metaphor of technology as a field in factor input space) is *not* technological advance is inextricably linked to the notion that substitution of one commodity for another is always available along a continuum of choice that varies with relative price. In both cases, real event-laden, irreversible time is eliminated; by the implicit assumption that the passenger pigeon scenario is always remediable with another resource that is always a perfect stand-in for the extinct one. We really can pass that way again, no matter what was done in the past. This makes the equilibrium–field metaphor utterly exogenous to the economics of the growth vs. development trade-off and its concern with the permanent impact of human economic behavior on the environment. (See the last section of Chapter six.)

The reader should consider the remarks of two well-known neoclassical economists including a well-known "paradigm-shifter" and the fatal contradiction it has lead into . . . without notice by the culprits: Who are hardly ever challenged about such matters from within the dominant "neoclassical" community of faith.

In *A Neo-classical Analysis of the Economics of Natural Resources*, Joseph Stigiltz (1979), described as a neoclassical economist, declared that: "Natural resources are basically no different from (i.e., are infinitely substitutable for) other factors of production."

Therefore from the premise of "infinite substitutability" other similar statements by such eminent neoclassical economists as Robert Solow (1974) are hardly surprising: "The world can, in effect, get along without natural resources."

Should these quotations be accepted as "advocacy" from the two academics quoted above, or merely as the "hot pursuit" of the neoclassical "paradigm" to its bitter end"?

This kind of mind set carries inside its entrails the grossest of inconsistencies—the belief in "infinite substitutability" is congruent with the cargo-cult "vision" of Technos as a "free good—an "exogenous shock" to the "standard model" of "steady-state equilibrium growth paths" where the most powerful form of human economic behavior—the Promethean imperative—is simply "collapsed" to a residual operator. But the quotations from two typical neoclassical practitioners (above) strongly imply that substitution is strongly rooted in technological innovation applied to selecting the factor-mixes employed in the productive technologies; It supplies the "getting along without natural resources" (Robert Solow). But the isoquant representation of the (pseudo) production function—the enshrined embodiment of "timelessness" in the neo-classical "paradigm"— proclaims explicitly that substitution is unambiguously excluded as a variety of technological improvement in the efficiency of production.

This is hardly their only experience of gross conflict with reality. See Chapter 5 on Capital for a much greater embarrassment (or is self-inflicted "paradox" more appropriate?): The "conclusion" reached by Jorgenson and Grilliches that there was no contribution to growth from technological change in American Industry between 1945 and 1967. Shades of TFP (Total Factor Productivity)! Perhaps the guilty parties should consult the *not*-forgotten wisdom of Ludwig Mises:

> Action (as in the Promethean Imperative) implies change: change implies (the notion of) temporal sequence—or (real event-laden)—Time. Human reason is even incapable of conceiving the very ideas of timeless action, or timeless existence.

or

The great Alfred Marshall's admonition, paraphrased: "Problems about how Time should be treated underlie most outstanding and unresolved issues in economic analysis." Most, if not all, contemporary economic literature is written as if the last 150 years of thinking about time and process never happened.

Chapter Four

Macro-Economic Consequences— Quantity of Work, Employment and Income Levels

The first man to found and *populate a market* town . . . was Phoroneus, son of the river-god Inachus and the nymph Melia. . . . Phoroneus was also the first to discover the *use* of fire, *after* Prometheus had stolen it. . . . Phoroneus's name is read by the Greeks as *"bringer of price"* in the sense that he invented *markets.* . . .

—*The Greek Myths*, Robert Graves, George Braziller, Inc. New York, 1959, Volume I, Chapter 57, Phoroneus . . . (See Appendix One)

For it is the *principle* of MACHINERY and not just its deadly chop-chop way of making goods that is uncongenial to the mind and the instincts. A MACHINE *is* a system, a *breeder* of system. It eliminates chance and like NUMBER itself, removes reality to replace it by abstraction. . . . The whole speculative, hypothetical character of modern economic life, its relentless fantasy, is implicit in the first MACHINE.

—Jacques Barzun, *Science, The Glorious Entertainment*, Harper and Row, 1964, Chapter III, Love and Hatred of the Machine, page 35.

Let us remember that the automatic machine . . . is the precise economic equivalent of slave labor. Any labor that competes with slave labor must accept the economic conditions of slave labor. It is perfectly clear that this will produce an unemployment situation in comparison with which . . . the depression of the '30s will seem a pleasant joke. This depression will ruin many industries—possibly even those industries that have taken advantage of the new potentialities."

—Norbert Wiener,
"The Human Use of Human Beings,"
Cybernetics and Society, 1950.

and finally

1955—A conversation between Henry Ford II and Walter Reuther, President of the United Auto Workers of America, while inspecting one of the first examples of an automated assembly line:

Henry Ford II, pointing to one of the automatons: "Look at those guys, Walter. *They'll* never go out on strike."

Walter Reuther: "Yeah, Henry, but *they'll* never buy your f . . . n' cars either."

For a more recent (1996) opinion on the subject, the reader should consult Appendix 4 of Chapter Three.

When technos, the Promethean Imperative, and Telos, (the aims, the goals, the purposes of economic activity and all the commodities, skills and tools associated with them) interact along the trajectory of technological time, they produce a succession of market "membranes" which may be "cut" into distinct eras. The history of such eras is the content of economic history. The most important *resultant* variables *for the human condition* which arise from such *path-dependent* interaction are:

1. The amount of *work actually required* in one market "membrane" or "era" of $\mathfrak{I}$ compared to the previous ones, in order to achieve the actual income levels that support the perceived standards of living, and to pursue ω-omega $\equiv$ CCSL (Current Conception of the Standard of Life) + Sector 2. This is called the *Natural Participation Rate,* or N_r for shorthand purposes. *It is a description of Labor needed, rather than:*

2. *Employment levels actually measured and recorded*, which is the *socially culturally, and institutionally determined distribution* of the *Natural* Participation Rate. This is determined by such factors as the income share distribution between capital and labor, the strength of labor unions, family and class structures, efficiencies of particular *markets* (very social institutions, ever since Phoroneus invented them), legal definitions of a maximum working day, child labor laws, participation of women in the labor force, retirement customs, ecological and environmental restrictions, prevailing attitudes toward the acceptance of debt and risk, et al.

3. Macro-economic Income levels.

Consider the Figure 4.1 below, which illustrates the *sequential flow* of the key macro-economic variables described above.

Figure 4.1 The Origins of the Labor Market

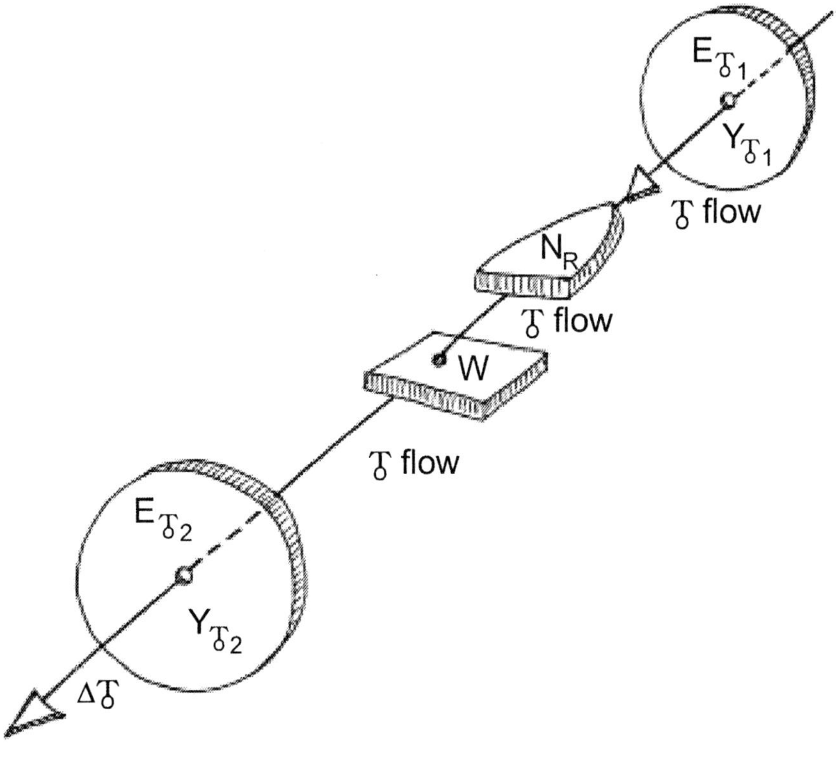

In Figure 4.1:

$E_{\mathcal{T}1}$ and $Y_{\mathcal{T}1}$ represent the employment level and (macro-economic) income level at $\mathcal{T}_1$

$\Delta'\mathcal{T}$ represents the flow (at varying rates) along the trajectory of technological time, which is *not* dead clock time, but event-laden "duree." This flow of Technological time, represented geometrically, embodies the principle that the events are the time. One of the earliest modern attempts to grapple with the great problem of real time in human affairs was that of Frederick Nietzsche. He admonished his readers to:

1. Think of things as events and families of events; The world consists only of events. It is necessarily formless and being formed at the same time.
2. Human wills are conceived as causing families of events. They are always acting upon each other. It is admittedly difficult to grasp a clear image of this chain of action of one will on another, in which form is imposed, event upon event.
3. Grasping things as events "simpliciter" is admittedly counter to common sense. Nevertheless, Nietzsche insists that we abandon the notion that events consist of things, items, or artifacts, and that events are merely the interaction between things. He is asking us to grasp the world as "families of events," as consisting of no-thing in particular—a world of interactive relations without "relata." The reader should consult Rudiger Safranski's superb biography of Nietzsche, published by Norton and Company, 2002, New York and London, ISBN 0-393-32380.

(The reader should consult Appendix 6, Chapter Three, and associated main text.)

N_r represents the natural participation rate that has formed along $\mathcal{T}$, at a certain point on its trajectory, as a consequence of the *process innovation* content of $\mathcal{T}$, expressed in terms of change in the stages of production or equivalents thereto. It is shown in lighter dotted lines because it is an authentic "virtual" entity, with operational impact, (see Appendix 2) but whose quantifiability is perpetually elusive. *It is the underlying reality of legitimate attempts to measure or estimate productivity change.* It is a macro-economic reality which cannot be arrived at by aggregating all its constituent and corresponding micro-economic productivity events. It is the very prototype of a gestalt entity in this respect, because the interrelationships of key economic variables that lead to productivity can be described with considerable accuracy in qualitative (including taxonomic) terms. It also accounts for the myriad (disparate?) attempts to find the perfect "proxy" for Technos, that fits neatly in time series and associated regressions that are compatible with a one to one correspondence between clock time and "progress" ≡ growth.

ω (and including the CCSL) represents the macro-economic Telos of economic society at a certain point along the trajectory of technological time. It is itself a virtual and profoundly gestalt entity because its interactions with both the *product* and *service* innovation content of Υ and perceptions of economically viable technological opportunities, can be qualitatively described with reasonable accuracy, but to aggregate it to a macro-economic magnitude from all the micro-economic and individual decisions behind the metamorphoses of the CCSL and Sector 2 of Telos (e.g., every threshold of consumption, every critical increment, every perception of *real* income and price change and their maelstrom of interactions. . . (see Chapter Two, Appendix 3) is inherently impossible . . . as similar phenomena in other social sciences. All that can be known about the macro-economic process, as it moves along its trajectory with its built-in lags between perception, cognitive adaptation, and the response of imperfect individuals and the imperfect institutions they rely on, (the heart of the hysteresis relationship at the macro-economic level) are the "unfolding" net results as embodied by employment, income, and gross output. Of all the markets that are formed from this path-dependant process, the most basic in its human consequences, and still the most perplexing, is the labor market. What are the ultimate causes of work and job creation, major fluctuations in demand for them, and of their often irreversible political and social consequences. To what extent are they really manageable by even the most well-intentioned and presumably sophisticated policies and "safety nets?" As John Stuart Mill once asked rhetorically and with deep understanding, "demand for commodities is not necessarily the demand for labor"? (It ought to be in a perfect Say's Law economy.) From the preceding text and Figure 4.1, the following *very* general statement can be made: The levels of employment and (macro) income that form during a current technological time, and which support the current observable standard of living, metamorphasized from the Natural Participation rate and operational Telos (CCSL and *Sector* 2) formed from earlier interactions with the flow of technological time.

i.e., $E_{\mho} = f\,(N_r \text{ at } \mho\text{-}1, \omega \text{ at } \mho\text{-}1$ 4.1

$Y_{\mho} = F(E_{\mho})$ 4.2

Since these are gestalt relationships, it is sufficient to describe their approximate interactive structural relationships. It is unrealistic and misleading, and not in the nature of the subject, to presume to a "higher" level of exactitude or quantifiability."

In Figure 4.1, the income and employment levels shown at $\mho_2$ happen to appear quantitatively greater than at $\mho_1$ (i.e., the pie-shaped representation of E and Y is bigger at $\mho_2$ than at $\mho_1$. Thus some degree of economic growth is illustrated in this *particular* case. But there is no inherent reason in a time-path–dependent economic process (one that is characterized by Veblenesque "unfolding" rather than automatically attained full employment equilibrium) why this optimistic scenario should be anything other than episodic at best. There are no guarantors of "warranted growth rates" or conservateurs of even pre-existing income and employment* levels; nor, consequently, will the goods and services that get to be produced and consumed at $\mho_2$ necessarily ever measure up to the CCSL that motivated economic behavior at a preceding technological time. Nor are prolonged periods of "glut" (classical term), "underemployment equilibrium" (neoclassical term), secular stagnation, deficiencies in the "warranted growth rate of income" (Harrod), necessarily paradoxical, not provable or explicable only in terms of such "perversities" of human nature as "stickiness," and accumulations of "rigidities."

Consider the following figures, 4.3 to 4.6 inclusive:

---

* The reader should consult Samuel Hollander's *The Classical Economists* (page 216) for J.S. Mill's concern with the same process. Would the normal employment of the same number of workers at roughly the same wages be conserved following a "labor saving" improvement (almost always referred to as "machinery" by the Victorians, and at the end of a 1933 movie called "Dinner at Eight" by Jean Harlow and Marie Dressler) in the technology of production?

When our readers use these figures they should ask themselves the following questions: To what extent does our approach embody Hayek's insights that general pattern prediction is far more appropriate to Economics than the spurious exactitude of trying for "precise" numerical quantity . . . as if economic phenomena are just like measurable physical substances . . . e.g., the "Monetarist Conceit" described in Chapter Five. The reader should compare this approach to the notorious "junk-science" proclamations of Maurice Allais & Paul Samuelson.

Maurice Allais, 1992: "The essential condition of any science is the existence of regularities which can be analyzed and forecast. This is the case with celestial mechanics . . . and true of economic phenomena . . . just as striking as those found in the physical sciences. Economics is a science which rests on the same general principles as physics." Not to be out-done, the venerable Samuelson had declared, "Physics and economics share the same general mathematical theorems" . . . and then he condemned Ludwig Edler Mises for his "A-priorism"! No wonder both John V. Neumann & Oskar Morgenstern had commented in the 1950s that "Samuelson has some rather murky ideas about stability."

Truly a classic of courteous understatement!

In Figure 4.3, employment levels and associated aggregate incomes are the only purely dependent variables generated by interactions of the flow of technological time ($\Delta \Upsilon$), the Natural Participation Rate (N_r) and the Operational Telos (ω) which includes the CCSL and Sector 2. The reader should keep in mind that N_r is the (gestalt) result of sensitivity to the *process* innovation content of Υ; Omega (ω) is more sensitive to *product* (and service) innovation and *perceptions* of technological opportunities as contents of technological time.

With due allowance for the inevitable loss of clarity when the interactions of four variables are *schematically* represented on a flat surface, suppose that the flow of Υ produces a movement from point A on N_r (Υ_1) to point B on Nr (Υ_2). At A an income level of $Y(\omega_1)$ corresponds to an employment level of E_1. But at B it corresponds to a *higher* income level, Y_2, associated with a *lower* employment level E_2.

Therefore, in order to have maintained the same level of employment, E_1, the operational Telos ought to have "expanded" to a "magnitude" ω_3, so that it would have generated an even higher level of income, $Y(\omega_3)$, for the maintained employment level E_1 at B_1. If the income share "balance of power" had remained the same, then a higher per capita income—which would have supported a resultant higher standard

Figure 4.3

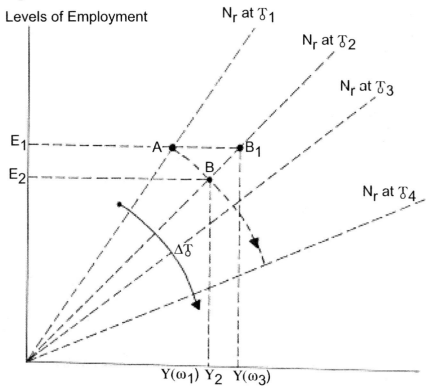

Gross Domestic Income Levels Associated With Varying
ω's $\rightarrow$ Operational Teloses (CCSL and Sector 2)

of living more appropriate to a superior $\mathcal{T}_2$—would have been generated,
thus bestowing greater prosperity on an unreduced *employed* labor force
. . . i.e., on the same number of job holders. For connoisseurs of Hume's
"Guillotine" this is a scenario where "is" has unfolded from "ought to."
This scenario could also be interpreted as an episodic appearance of the
consequences of the "law" of "automatic compensation" and a vindica-
tion of the "insatiability" of consumption wants, which underlies Say's
law.

But at point B the universe has not unfolded quite the way it ought to.
A higher per capita income has been generated for a level of employment
E_2 that may be described as "degenerate" with respect to E_1. What could
have happened between point A and point B to the *responses* of remain-

Figure 4.4

Employment Levels

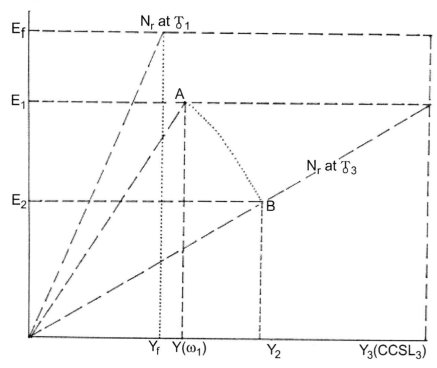

Gross Domestic Income Levels

ing job holders and those who make the key economic decisions in the institutions of both the private and public sectors? In terms of the Telos-Technos nexus, specifically as described in Chapter 2, nothing that is deviant from the nature of *homo aeconomus* or from the normal behavior of his institutions, that is, hysteresis, non-automatic, contingency-loaded behavior, the inevitable lag times of cognitive adaptation, along the trajectory of evolutionary time.

But it could have been better. Consider Figure 4.4.

Consider a very large change in the Natural Participation rate from A to B; i.e., from N_r at $\mathcal{T}_2$ to N_r on $\mathcal{T}_3$. Then initially the employment level falls to E_2. This means that a lesser number of job holders earn a larger aggregate income, and consequently now have significantly larger per capita incomes. But the newly unemployed ($E_1 - E_2$) will have their per capita incomes reduced to that provided by social assistance, unemployment benefits, and sundry other transfer payments. Therefore the reaction from the consumption accumulation process rests entirely with the remaining job holders, disregarding for the moment the reactions of those decision makers in Sector 2 of Telos. But we are in a state of "fundamental optimism about the ability of the economy to re-absorb labor" (See Appendix 4, Chapter 3) or what amounts to the same thing believe in the law of automatic compensation with its full retinue of perfectly synchronized income and substitution effects. Thus, the employed residual of the labor force, E_2, will have such a robust, insatiable appetite for greater consumption that the employment level will be quickly restored to its former level, E_1, corresponding to a greatly enhanced income level, Y_3, associated with the insatiably robust $CCSL_3$; and, of course, a full menu of product and service innovations will have appeared magically in the "field" of consumers' vision, that will experience no cognitive lag times in breaking through whatever thresholds of consumption might delay or even stop them from being chosen; and the greatly enhanced real income levels have generated a chain of critical increments that would easily "mow them down," so to speak (See Chapter 2 and Appendix 5). Indeed, one other variation in this movement to super prosperity afforded by the steep decline in the N_r could be mopping up of any unemployed job seekers that existed prior to E_1 as a consequence of the very general relationships in Chapter 2, (1) to (6). . . . $E_{full\ employment}$ that existed when N_r at $\mathcal{T}_1$ prevailed on the trajectory of macro-economic time. This process of absorption would probably have entailed some minor adjustments in the average length of customary workdays and overtime, as institutional inspired shifts in the distribution of changing N_r's and incomes (and their resultant "automatic" enhancements of aggregate demand) unfold. Thus the best of all possible worlds has occurred: full employment at greatly augmented levels of personal and aggregate prosperity, right up to the full potential of technological time.

   Having examined two of many possible scenarios that are of the "positive" kind, let us now proceed to a somewhat less positive scenario. Consider a scenario (Figure 4.5, where the N_r falls from A at $\mathcal{T}_1$ to B at $\mathcal{T}_2$. Therefore, initially employment falls from E_1 to E_2, but with increased aggregate income level Y_2, just like the preceding scenario *to this point*. Suppose however that the current conception of the standard of life (CCSL) is, for various reasons, very sluggish rather than being

Figure 4.5

Employment Levels

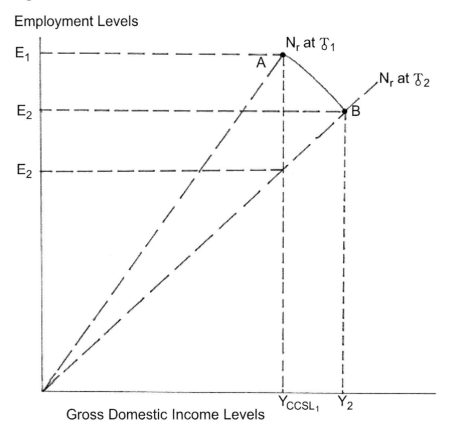

Gross Domestic Income Levels

propelled forward by an "insatiable" and perfectly phased automatic appetite for commodities. Perhaps the amount and quality of product innovation being perceived cannot clear enough thresholds of consumption (i.e., Category 2 of the CCSL is not very active). Perhaps non-economic events lead to a stronger (precautionary) propensity to save; perhaps the marginal propensity to save is not quite so "constant" and so forth (see Chapter 2 of Appendix 3 and Appendix 1 of Chapter 4). Does this mean that the level of employment will simply settle down to some form of weak equilibrium (presumably one of many such "rest points in decision space") such that in this particular one the employment level E_2 is degenerate with respect to E_1 but aggregate Y_2 is decidedly superior to Y (ω_1)?*

At this point, depending on the percentage weight of the unemployed who were not automatically absorbed by the "insatiable" consumption appetites of the remaining job holders, or the degree of generosity of unemployment benefits, or "make-work" projects in the public sector, etc., the average incomes of the entire labor force, employed and otherwise, has fallen, and are perceived to have done so by both the individuals and institutions *who constitute the decision-making marketplace*. Referring back to relationships in Chapter 2, 1 to 6 inclusive, the subsequent formations of decisions affecting *consumption* and associated investment, are strongly affected by perceptions of income change during a preceding period and "expectations" for the future. Thus a chain of increasingly weaker CCSLs has been generated because of a "grandfathered" weak response having cumulated from the original A to B decrease in the Natural participation rate.

The end result of this contagious debilitation of the consumption accumulation process and associated investment activity, *even if the operational telos/CCSL gets no worse than CCSL_1* (the "best of the worst" scenario), is the formation of both a degenerate employment level, E_3, *and* the beginning point of a declining sequence of degenerate aggregate income levels.

They are termed degenerate because not only is employment at E_3 even lower than it was at E_1 *and* E_2; aggregate income has now fallen back to that associated with $CCSL_1$ *from* Y_2; put another way, the income level associated with E_3 is degenerate because not only is it lower

---

* The flow of $\mathfrak{T}$ has, in this case, redistributed income shares. The origins of these changes can be traced directly to specific changes in "process innovation" interacting with responsive choices in the CCSL and perhaps sector 2 of Omega (ω)—whether strong, weak, or not at all. All this myriad complexity of what is, in effect, quite systematic human behavior is of a gestalt nature. It cannot be "aggregated" in "arithmomorphic" (Georgescu Roegen's term) fashion to a definite cardinal "quantity"; although the attempts to do so by many outstanding figures (Wesley Clair Mitchell) should never have been so disparaged by some of the "Austrian" school economists, despite their loathing of the "Positivist" roots of both him and his colleagues. Men (and women) long for precision in their zeal to "score" economic performance. It seems much easier at the individual level than at the societal one!

than it ought to have been if even E_2 had been maintained at N_r associated with $\mathfrak{T}_2$ (i.e., Y_2); it had even fallen back to $Y_{CSL\ 1}$ with no guarantees it could not fall back further with the flow of $\mathfrak{T}$—a bleak scenario indeed, but not impossible. This scenario clearly corresponds to that of Norbert Wiener, quoted at the beginning of Chapter 4 (See Appendix 1).

Consider one more scenario with the $N_r/\mathfrak{T}$ configuration, keeping in mind that *only the general direction of movement* arising from *contingent* economic behavior and the *estimated* consequences of interactions of associated variables is being illustrated. No further extension of this method into presumably more impressive levels of quantifiability and exactitude is justifiable, however tempting. In this case more modest rates in the flow of technological time are described and the job holding labor force resulting from associated change in the N_r, responds reasonably well, but not *automatically* or "*insatiably*" to the new opportunities for consumption expansion offered via Category 2 of the $CCSL_1$).

Initially E_1 recedes to E_2 associated with a slightly higher level of aggregate income and a correspondingly increased level of per capita

Figure 4.6

Employment Levels

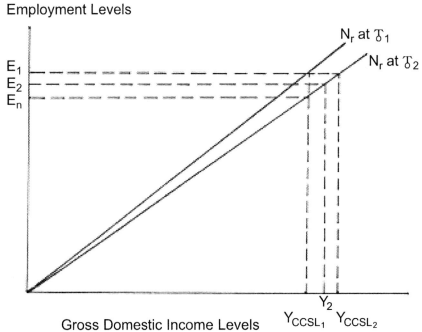

Gross Domestic Income Levels Y_{CCSL_1} Y_{CCSL_2}

income. (Note that if the movement of N_r from $\mho_n$ to $\mho_{n+1}$ is represented by a straight line "drop" instead of the "swing" of an arc downwards, the average level of income would have increased to $Y_{CCSL\ 1}$, $\div E_n$.) But the economic interpretation of such different representations probably rests with different institutionally handled distributions of increased capacity-for-wealth creation.

In this case, referring to Figure 4.6, in order to re-absorb $E_1 - E_2$ back into the ranks of job-holders, the response of job holders E_2 with (interim) aggregate income level of Y_2 should move the economy forward to $Y_{CCSL\ 2}$. By experimenting with various manipulations of this configuration, taking care not to presume to any degree of accuracy beyond that inherent in the subject variables, it is possible to build up a consistent series of corresponding "eras" of economic history to particular states of the preceding configuration (See Appendix 1 again). For example, just after World War II, most reputable economists predicted a major depression that, in retrospect, was a nearly perfect fit to the Norbert Wiener scenario and Figure 4.5. Instead, a situation much closer to that depicted in Figure 4.4 actually materialized. The explanations for this widely unanticipated prosperity filled almost as many libraries as those explaining the Great Depression of the 1930s, but almost all of them wound up with some variation on the theme of "pent-up demand." Subsequent literature which attempted to explain post-war economic history usually revolved around such themes as "have we abolished the business cycle" or will the "challenge of affluence" ruin the character of consumers by inflaming their "insatiable need for commodities."

On this basis we can classify the "predictors" as to whether they are playing the role of Savonarola or Pollyanna. (See Chapter 3, Appendix 4). The reader should consult *William Vickrey's* observation of the rarity (historically) of the utopian state of "Full Employment of All Available Resources" (1926 and World War II).

From the preceding text, one conclusion is obvious. The macroeconomic process is *non-tautological* and cannot be adequately described as a (discontinuous) succession of ("multiple") equilibrium states, rather like randomly discovered milestones with no road linking them.

It is *non*-tautological because the chances of winding up with the same *resultant* standard of living as was envisaged by the original operational Telos, earlier in the "trajectory" of economic history, may be described as episodic at best. The flow of Technological time and its manifestation in the N_r, coupled with less than "appropriate" responses in the CCSL or Sector 2 of ω, may cause difficulty in the ability of subsequently resultant purchasing power to buy up to even a previous established "standard of living." And on occasion a resultant standard of living further along the trajectory of economic history may exceed anything that was ever envisaged. (Sometimes economic history exists only as subjective juxtapositions in the eye of the beholder.) However, once the straitjacket of the Say/Walras Boundary conditions and the "law" of automatic compensation (J.R. McCulloch) are removed—which are legitimate and consistent up to a level of explanation which culminated in the Heuristic Programming "revolution" (post-war development of World War II operations Research)—then the contingent nature of economic history becomes apparent.

and

There cannot be any "iron laws" that *determine* the "path" of economic history. Such "prophecy" is more in the nature of proclamation, disguised as "Science" that was so typical of 19th Century crack-pot determinists, from Gobineau to Marx to Houston Stuart Chamberlain and their disciples in the twentieth century. Their "predictive power" was closer to Nostradamus than to Darwin. Their powers of explanation were closer to those who can explain "the price of everything and the value of nothing." Economic behavior is contingent and value-loaded and has a gestalt relationship to the consequences of its own interactions. Therefore no strictly "determined" rest point or steady-state, whatever we choose to call it, can be the result of a process which originates in human behavior at the individual level, or that of their institutions which are governed by "rules" crafted by groups of individuals. Unless they are "Lotus eaters" (see Appendix 1 again) they started off with particular sets of teloses, or envisaged "ends"—which, in the course of those actions to which they "bear a causal relationship" ("Austrian" economics' talk), may be achieved, missed, or even surpassed.

The process described in this chapter reveal the limits of macro-intervention, or even synthesizing economic activity by "positivist" oriented planning from the "top" which includes "monetarism" (see Chapter 5, The "Monetarist" Conceit): AND—certainly tends to support Hayek's warnings: As an economy becomes more and more complex (recall his differentiation between complex science and the more "physical" sciences) the number of ways that we can intervene without negative unintended consequences, becomes more and more constricted. AND—

A knowledge of limitations is, in itself, a significant advance in human knowledge. This insight has direct application to the Telos-Technos nexus. The gestalt principle is the insistent operational limitation to frustrated aspirations for a mathematical exactitude comparable to those of 19th century energy physics. It is inherent in the nature of our subject and precludes the chimera of perfect aggregatibility from the micro to the macro levels. Note that the great Hayek did not use the word "information" in this context. He used "knowledge" because this concept incorporates understanding of the world. "Information" still partakes of its cybernetic definition: Whatever is transmitted from A to B . . . period. The explanation advanced in this chapter should not, however, be interpreted as an argument against any intervention in the economy by any level of government at all. That degree of "laissez-faire" could in many circumstances lead to "spontaneous order" manque—the very pathological instability that so many ill-begotten governances of the last century unleashed on the world . . . and whose baleful consequences have not yet been remedied. Navigating the zone between these two poles has indeed become more and more uncertain.

Appendix 1

For connoisseurs of economic interpretations derivable from the "myths" (?) of the ancient Greeks, we should also turn to Homer's Odyssey for his version of authentic "shock" to purposeful human action. The **Lotus** (opium?) **Eaters**. Under extremely unusual but entertaining circumstances, Odysseus' (Ulysses') crew had abandoned their particular obligations that arose from the "gestalt-drag" on their Promethean Imperative; it had generated intensely teleological behavior . . . working toward goals, whether modest or grandiose, hedonistic (as in the CCSL) or adventurous. Obviously, old Homer thought that the absence of the Promethean imperative was the most contemptible "shock" to the human condition—perfect "stasis," an equilibrium, a "rest" point from which no human action, economic or otherwise, can be generated.

The "moral" of the "story"?

Phoroneus is to Prometheus as Telos is to Technos . . .
The evolution of markets is the active (institutional) expression of human teleologies.

Teleologies ≡ the "matrix" of ends.

Technos → Technological Time → the "matrix" of "means"

Appendix 2

A quite recent hypothesis regarding the possible lack of automatic symmetry between the "process innovation" aspect of technological change and its product innovation aspect, is put forward by Rick Szotak in *Technological Innovation and the Great Depression*—Boulder and Oxford Harper Collins, Westview Press, 1995.
His hypothesis is that the lengthy downturn was caused by

an abundance of labor-saving technological change coupled with a virtual absence of new product innovation. . . . Saturation would not have been that serious a problem if consumers had new consumption outlets—i.e., new products to buy . . . paucity of new products or industries in the years *prior to* the 1930s.

Two key elements of his hypothesis are:

1. "New products have a higher elasticity of demand than older ones." (See Appendix 3 of Chapter 2, Technos and Telos, which dates from 1967, *Re*: shapes of demand curves.)
2. "Process innovations . . . have a much lower impact on overall demand than product innovations." Mr. Szotak's hypothesis is very interesting indeed and is reasonably capable of being tested, using the material from Chapter 2 especially, which dates from 1967, and Chapter 4 as well.

. . . Based on review of book in *Journal of Economic Literature,* Fall, 1997.

Appendix 3

Perceptions about the Natural Participation Rate, including estimates about its *existing* trends, and projections of its future impact, are the routine ingredients of decisions about personnel and labor needs by all kinds of executives, line management production supervisors, etc. It is a kind of "current" conception of future labor requirements. "Such prognosticating is not so different in spirit than those described in Chapter 3, by the "Think Tanks" and roundly condemned and then subsequently practiced by George Orwell.

A possible direction for "thought experiment" involving the N_r concept would suggest such juxtapositions as:

1. Try to estimate what percentage of the *present* labor force, *using the clerical technologies of 1940*, would be required to handle the data processing "requirements" of the late 1990s. Would the "requirements" have arisen in the first place if not for perfectly natural, and *not unexpected* perceptions about the capabilities of modern clerical technology to process such requirements." How much of this "requirement" reflects "Parkinson's Law" rather than the "Law" of Supply and Demand for labor?

2. Estimate what percentage of the *1950* labor force would be required to service the demand for agricultural products, (using the Υ's of 1950 and 1995 respectively) for the market of 1995. What percentage of the 1995 labor force would be needed to service the agricultural products needs of 1970?

Chapter Five

Capital

Capital is indisputably one of the very few key operational concepts of economic thought and also the most elusive and controversial. Indeed, the ideological and academic conflicts revolving around capital (theory and practice) are infamous for generating "more heat than light." Yet much first class thinking has, historically, gone into the subject and permanently valuable insights are *not* rare from the classical economists, through the Austrian School to the ideas of the Cambridge (United Kingdom) "School," and their United States colleagues.

The treatment of the nature of capital in this chapter will build on the best insights from the past, concentrating not so much on their controversial aspects, as on their original intent; continuity with the ideas described by a Telos-Technos nexus will be emphasized where comparable; where they may not have any substantial linkage to important historic ideas on the subject, or conflict with them, will be left to the reader's judgement.

The material in this chapter will be very broadly based on the following topics:

1. An "axiomatic" acceptance of Sraffa's principle that, apart from relating the "quantity" or value of capital to the rate of profit and interest, there can be no such entity as an homogeneous, technical unit of capital that is (absolutely) aggregatable along a continuum, and may be simplistically comparable to any other aggregation of "capital" units through time, and manipulated as if it were.

    . . . and a similar acceptance that:

2. "Capital is what capital does" (Joan Robinson) and by extension, capital is what investment buys at a particular $\mathfrak{T}$ or *during* a particular technological "era," if such can be "cut" meaningfully (see Chapter Three).

3. Capital is a complex *heterogeneous* entity that functions in a number of *classifiable forms* as parts of interactive ensembles. Because of its heterogeneity and complexity, a taxonomic approach is the most operationally meaningful.

4. The value of particular forms (classified) of capital is directly related to and varies with Technological time. Indeed, its very identification as "capital" is intensely temporal. "Today's capital may be decomposed (imputed back through $\mathfrak{T}$echnological time) to yesterday's labor." But it takes its real, virtual value from what it does, in ensembles and with other factor inputs, *today*—i.e., historic "crystallized" labor content has little operational meaning *today* other than in its "rough and ready" Ricardian sense, and without regard to its "scarcity" value at particular points along the trajectory of economic history. $\mathfrak{T}$ may be thought of as a kind of "operator," on a given capital ensemble, "the operand."

5. The capital-output ratio is the most important derivative concept from "capital" particularly so because of its extreme sensitivity to technological time and its interaction with the savings-income ratio, i.e., the capital-output ratio is more closely co-related with technos; the savings income ratio is more sensitive to telos (the CCSL) and extra-economic and security concerns, or what Veblen called the non-economic parts "of the conscious life." Recall that Veblen warned against "isolating" economic phenomena from other aspects of the "conscious life." This advice has real operational meaning in a Telos-Technos nexus.

6. Certain *classifiable forms* of capital have more "conservateur" power than others, i.e., they are more endurable with respect to the "erosion" of technological time—more resistant to creeping obsolescence. The Shivic principle of "creative destruction" (Schumpeter) emerges much more clearly and with operational meaning when it is allowed to be heterogeneous, but Taxonomically organized as with Technology.

But what is the dividing line between "capital saving" and erosion of capital value?

What Capital is Not

If an entity is not homogeneous and stubbornly resists being treated as such by throwing off all manner of inconsistency, conflict, and controversy over an extended period of time, in spite of the best efforts of well intentioned and capable devotees of the subject, then perhaps it is timely to treat as heterogeneous, and to develop and *follow through on all the implications of this conclusion*; this is especially true of "capital" because of the efforts of Sraffa. After most of a lifetime's career pondering the subject he came as close as is logically possible to proving directly, rather than by trial and error and inductive efforts, that this key concept is otherwise intractable—especially when *forced* into the role of an homogeneous variable. The most interesting of such efforts, and perhaps the most well-intentioned in terms of complementing the equilibrium "paradigm," was the notion of "vintages" of capital. Another motive for introducing this notion was probably—to at least acknowledge the role of time in economic thought by paying it lip service—in the form of pseudo-dynamizing it. In this regard, the failure of the neoclassical school to even address the problem was honored more in the breach than the observance. Vintage models of capital are essentially an attempt to grope for a time-sensitive variation in a key variable that must somehow "conserve" its homogeneous nature, without which it can play no role in an equilibrium/field representation of macro-economics. Arguably one cannot even refer to an equilibrium/field representation as a "process." However, this is just the beginning of the confusion and controversy. After all the neoclassical perspective has a boundary value described in our terms as $\Upsilon = k$, or $\Delta\Upsilon = 0$ (i.e., it doesn't flow). That is, technology is exogenous to, or outside "The Scope and Methodology of Political Economy"—John Nivelle Keynes, i.e., if capital can be forced into a role as a physical unit of measurable substance, timelessly absolute, it can be aggregated along a continuum into a seamless (non-gestalt-like) whole; in this way it would behave itself dependably in micro-production functions which could, in principle, all be aggregated to one great "aggregate production function;" this is consistent with the frequent observation that absolute homogeneity (of an essentially heterogeneous entity) is a "must" in neoclassical theory. Another interesting benefit of this theoretical straitjacket is that a "mature" technology could be characterized by a scenario in which differences in the marginal productivities of successive vintages of capital become less and less positive. However the "vintage" approach generates an impressive casualty list in terms of empirical reality consistency, and inadequacy, in its picture of political economy as the consequences of human behavior.

1. It implies strongly that technical progress is, for the most part, "embodied" in successively superior models of physical capital, i.e., "machinery" as the classical economists called it:

    and by extension that

2. There is a one-to-one correspondence between the passage of chronological time and technical progress; this amounts to little more than a crude statement that technical progress is automatic—perhaps even spontaneously generated! In some such models the authors are candid enough to state these assumptions "up-front;" but even if they don't bother, these built-in assumptions usually come out the other end, proving once again that growth in an economy along "stable equilibrium growth paths" requires a one-to-one correspondence between the passage of chronological time and investment in technical progress.
3. A vintage embodiment of technical progress loses the sense of cognitive continuity in human economic behavior (See Figure 3.2 and subsequent text).
4. Since capital is a timeless, homogeneous, quantifiable physical unit and since it interacts with homogeneous labor in many finite micro-production functions, which in turn may be "aggregated" into one great "aggregate production function," it follows that technological progress's contribution to growth is, at last in principle, perfectly dissectable from that of brute accumulation of physical capital (See Appendix 1). It is not surprising, therefore, that on more than a few occasions such a paradigm (is parody a better term?) has led to some rather startling conclusions. For example:

In a 1967 article by D.W. Jorgenson and Z. Griliches, it was concluded that the "value" of capital grew entirely because of "accumulation" and consequently that no technical progress had occurred in United States industry since 1945. ("The Explanation of Productivity Change," *Review of Economic Studies*, 34, July 1967. See Appendix 1 again.)

A more recent and equally intriguing development during the 1990s has been the rise of what may be termed "hyper-embodiment" models of growth. The gist of this approach is that the economic "process" is largely a matter of applying varying "quantities" (??) of Capital and "Knowledge" to a fixed "quantity" of *labor*, presumably homogeneous (see Appendix 5.2). One last example of many is the representation of business cycles as the consequences of "exogenous technology shocks" to the "Solow residual" causing departure from "its steady state growth path." Such models also contain much reference to "perturbations" and "impact periods" perhaps reflecting an extension of the energy physics metaphor (mid-19th century vintage) to an Astro-physics metaphor. "Technology shock" is occasionally credited with its own "internal . . . laws of motion."

Ironically enough, (for the pacifists and moralists among us) one of the rarest and clearest examples of a simple application of the constant vintage principle occurred in the Korean War. Assuming that the military "labor" on both the United Nations side (mostly American or United States allies) and the Chinese was more or less "homogeneous," the following "logistical" strategy was followed by the United States Joint Chiefs of Staff: Knowing that the Chinese Red Army enjoyed a significant numerical advantage, without the need to change from a land-to-water and back-to-land medium, the American Command lavishly endowed their forces with the indisputably "constant vintage" military capital of World War II's final stages—late model propellor aircraft, early marks of jet aircraft, the same artillery park, shoulder arms, tanks, jeeps, etc.

The Chinese Red Army, according to a wealth of data and accounts of surviving veterans, had little more than shoulder arms and light mortars and machine guns. Most of their supply infrastructure was unmotorized. Militarily at least, the Chinese suffered a stunning defeat in spite of initial successes from November of 1950 to January of 1951, attributed largely to the element of surprise (to General MacArthur anyway) and mass momentum. Arguably, the first casualty of a commitment to the vintage-homogeneous capital method is evident from Figures 3.3 to 3.5 and was pointed out by Joan Robinson and others in Cambridge

(U.K.). The practitioners of this type of analysis had inadvertently staggered into an embarrassingly circular mode of thought. How could the *same* "quantity" of something called "capital" be a cause of increasingly greater productivity, in which case the capitals involved must have "embodied" unequal, not the *same* powers of causation? Yet they remained somehow homogeneous and equal . . . et al. The same acrobatics used to get around this anomaly, which involved the circularity of capital (openly made congruent with "equipment") values and adjustments to a desired result, via "well-cooked" rates of capitalization, need not concern us here. But even on their own, they constitute the best single argument for Technological time and the organized (=taxonomic) approach to heterogeneous capital.

If "capital is what capital does" (Joan Robinson), and capital is indisputably a heterogeneous entity, then the different forms and classes of capital do different things which are nevertheless sufficiently similar *in intent* to come under the same general rubric. One of the attributes that binds them together in this way is the designated term for the money that buys "capital," i.e., investment. A given amount of money may buy exactly the same product and service in one context, and be called a consumer purchase; in another context it would be classified as an investment. For example, 100 man-hours of electricians' service and associated materials may be a stage of production in manufacturing refrigerated truck trailers and in a recreational motorized yacht. Yet the former expenditure is classified as capital and the latter as a consumer durable. In the light of the Telos-Technos nexus, and assuming that the monetary expenditure was the same, it is obvious that calling the same purchase "capital" in the former case and (part of the CCSL) a *consumers'* durable in the latter, reflected the economic telos of the transactions . . . built into the very language (see quotation from Veblen at the beginning of Chapter 2, and the "Black Box Technology" table in Chapter 3). In other words, a description of the dollar quantities expended—and even the services and materials purchased—is inadequate (see Appendix 5.3). Thus the late Professor Robinson's aphorism was profoundly teleological . . . even "Veblenesque." We may go so far as to state that *not* classifying capital, and not building some degree of teleological thinking into the taxonomy, is equivalent to leaving a "veil" of inadequate description (only a monetary number) in its wake . . . little better than the construct of "homogeneous" capital. But a taxonomic system for capital that builds telos into its classifications is also profoundly path dependent, because it allows for preservation of its role as an agent . . . an enabler in a process of irreversible change while allowing it to change its content productivity and structure as a consequence of being transformed by Technological time in what is generically an operator-operand relationship—an image that owes much to Samuel Alexander's vision of the core-boring action of real event-composed time on materiality, which results in "emergences," *transformations of kind*, in quantity of variety, which are gestalt-like: like Henri Bergson's "novelty" . . . in contrast to simple quantitative change of the *same* distinct elements.

Towards a Taxonomy of Capital

If an expert in military logistics were to assess the strength and needs of any part of his nation's armed forces in terms of *only* the monetary values supplied to the budget committees of his government, he would be mercilessly discharged from his duties and no pronouncement of his would ever be taken seriously again. Even in the domain of heuristic programming, the applications that work best do so in industrial processes, where the ensembles of factor inputs are comparatively few, and can be easily labeled and quantified without resort to the various operations that must be used to standardize monetary values that mean different things through changing times and venues—i.e., they are confined to one "membrane" eras cut out of technological time (see Figure 3.6 and text following).

   While it is not realistic or feasible (just as is the case with "technos") to attempt to present a definitive taxonomy of capital all in one gulp, certain broad guidelines are evident from nearly two centuries of hard thinking on the subject.

1. There is no one form of capital that should dominate one's thinking to the point that this form alone becomes synonymous with all capital in much the same way that certain brand names of a particular class of product are used to designate the whole product category, e.g. "Kleenex" for all soft tissue paper. "Xerox" for all photo-copiers . . . and even elevated to a verb for all photo-copying, etc.
   In the heat of controversy there is a natural tendency to talk as if all capital is somehow embodied in "machinery," equipment, or (capital) "goods" or that "capital" is somehow generically interchangeable with *all* monies that are controlled

by a class of people called "capitalists" and who may choose not to use it for consumer expenditures at a particular time— or more to the point, withhold it from those who do. Even the most astute sometimes slip into such expediencies unintentionally.

2. The various forms of capital operate in ensembles, not only with labor, but in interactions with each other. It is a rare economic process indeed that involves only one form of capital. Indeed, in day-to-day business and accounting terms several categories of capital are identified with sufficient clarity to constitute, at the very least, a jumping off point for a more revealing and precise taxonomy. For example, the various forms of inventory peculiar to each industry; capital goods/ equipment; the most ancient and important form of inventory, seed grains and breeding stock; "goods in process," raw materials, working capital, fixed capital, infrastructure, etc. In addition, there is the peculiar contribution of economists—"human capital." The reader should consult John Stewart Mill on this subject. In *Principles of Political Economy*, 1848, he noted that "The acquired skills of the artisan are in principle a kind of capital in themselves . . . just like the machinery and tools they use." The reader should then consider whether the class of capital called Human Capital is even compatible with the notion of homogeneous labor, so necessary to the legitimacy of the various kinds of production functions? Indeed, just as in applying taxonomic principles to classifying technologies (Chapter Three), there is a need to use qualitative description to classify labor. The various standard classifications of industry and labor used by government and business for more than a century are as good a starting point as any. If liberalized to those forms of capital which are designed solely to improve our state of physical comfort to a point where we can work in a far more alert and efficient manner, they can themselves "embody" physical capital without being congruent with it: e.g., air conditioning, clear artificial light, and clean running water with inside plumbing. A working taxonomy of capital would reveal that these latter items are something more than contributors to a better "quality of life" or just capital goods and infrastruc-

ture. Indeed, air conditioning, modern ventilation systems, and water supply utilities make it possible to produce in locations where it was not previously possible to even live . . . human *enabling* capital if ever there was such, but not the only form of "human" capital. A good working classification system should reveal where distinct, heterogeneous forms of capital can "overlap" in particular ensembles without losing their particular identities.

3. When capital is classified, it is really being "de-homogenized," so to speak. The purpose for doing so is to identify the most elementary and distinct categories of capital so that what each does in its own right will emerge out of the "porridge" of "homogeneous" capital (see Appendix 5.4). It might be possible to identify a category of capital which is as close as anything can get to an economic "catalyst" through such a thinking process. We might also conjecture if taxonomic thinking—as opposed to make-believe homogeneous variables—would establish the existence and role of "preservative" forms of capital which in themselves comprise other sub-classes already familiar in previously identified ensembles. For example, the principle of "retrofit," modification, upgrading etc., not only prolongs the viable usage of other forms of capital. It can also reduce the cost of accumulating similar "vintages" of the capital being "modified." In the language of the"Austrian School," it thereby prevents the unnecessary lengthening of the period of production.

One One last comment on the usage of the word "capital" in the nineteenth and early twentieth century is necessary in the context of how to fit the concept of human capital (see Appendix 5.5) into a taxonomic approach to the subject. A particularly ingenious idea or a proposal that had economic potential was often referred to as a "capital" idea or as just plain "capital." This earlier language usage leads directly into the modern concept of Tacit Knowledge (F. Hayek and Michael Polanyi) which was described in Chapter Three as playing a major role in a class of events called *Substitution*. This is the very stuff of creative adaptation, on-the-spot alertness, and performed within the existing "state of the art" as defined in that chapter. The idea of capital as a form of superior or even unique knowledge that could be turned into profit has always been among those who best appreciate the Promethean imperative or its ancestral concept, the "instinct of workmanship."

Capital does not "embody" technology . . . Technological time operates on each and every class of capital and transforms them each in its own way, especially with regard to their *value* and kind, in the ensembles in which they act as factors of production.* If capital could "embody" technos, then the heterogeneous nature of capital could be squeezed back into the neoclassical straitjacket of one-form homogeneity. Put another way, one of the most important constituent interactions of $\mathcal{T}$ is technos circulating through and permeating the various classes of capital on a more or less continuous basis and at varying rates (see Appendix 5.6). This is really the operational rationale for developing the best possible classification system for capital—*as an "enabler" of the "capital is what capital does" principle*—without falling into the sterile trap of trying to manipulate capital as if it were a homogeneous (and therefore truly "scientific"?) measurable unit of physical substance . . . a lethal "hidden axiom" as defined by John Stewart Mill in his capacity as a logician, which has leeched the credibility out of the construct of Total Factor Productivity (TFP—Kendrick, circa 1960) . . . instead of the insistently and richly heterogeneous process it really is. In this regard, the readers should hearken back to the climax of the "Cambridge capital controversy," circa 1970. The combatants in Cambridge Mass. fabricated just such a concoction . . . LEETS! See the *Canadian Journal of Economics* article in the bibliography to this chapter.

Consider Figure 5.1 and subsequent discussion below:

Surface A represents all the "elements," consumption as well as capital, that constitute the latest output of an economy, i.e., of the first fiscal year. For the sake of illustration, capital elements are represented as black squares, consumption elements as white squares. Consider the element on surface A designated as a_t . Suppose we trace all the historic factor inputs that led up to the production of a_t on surface A. By means of this illustrative scheme we can *in principle* trace the economic genealogy

---

* Different "eras" of Technological time may well be characterized by different "class" mixes of capital. That is why, in the case of *Capital* a good "consensual" taxonomy would probably reveal far more about how (as in "means") change in the capital "stock," as Veblen meant it (see Appendix 5.8) contributes to economic change.

Figure 5.1

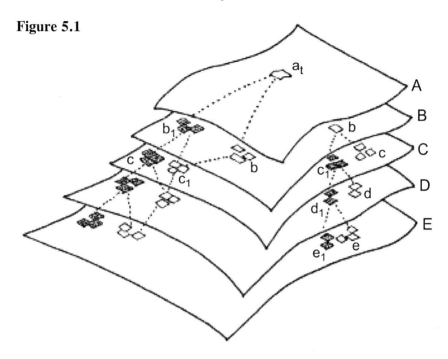

of a_t "back to Adam," so to speak; or alternatively it can represent a re-statement of J.S. Mill's breakdown of "fixed" capital into the wages of labor advanced in the past. If we trace the genealogy upwards from E to A, then in some sense we are tracing the economic and technological history of a_t from the first paw-grasped unaltered rock to the most con-temporary, state of the art robotic machine tool.

Therefore on surface B, one generation behind surface A, a block of labor elements b and a block of capital elements b_1 constitute the imme-diate factor "ancestry" of a_t. Similarly, blocks of labor and capital c and c_1 contributed to the sustenance and production of b and b_1, from gen-eration C to generation B, so to speak.

Of necessity there are certain very basic assumptions built into Fig-ure 5.1. There is an implicit presence of both homogeneous labor and homogeneous capital in every generation and there are no generations where the factor called capital is not somehow present. (The capitalists ye will always have amongst thee in thy land, so to speak)

In short, yesterday's labor is today's capital; today's labor is to-morrow's capital; today's capital saving is tomorrow's labor saving, etc. Of course, such a conception of capital is most comfortable when capital is embodied in "machinery" or is in some sense "fixed," as Mill well understood. And if it is the path of least resistance to explain technical change as somehow being most observable in such capital goods, the temptation to turn capital into a homogeneous *conservateur* that can be compared smoothly through time is irresistible. Who wants to deal with the painful, empirically obvious reality of heterogeneous capital, whose true nature only unfolds after it has been reduced and classified in the most "economic" way; and the most prototypical of its interactions are also identified and traced through economic and technological history? In this sense, neoclassical economic thought tried to take an illicit short-cut by skipping over the "reductionist" stage of the subject's develop- ment and simply adopting a counterfeit "holism" first, which manifested itself in an addiction to "homogeneous" variables which had never been subjected to "a critical account of all these quantitative notions and the means adopted for collecting and measuring them" (—Norbert Wiener; see Chapter Three, "A Modest Proposal"). What is being proposed here is to substitute "classify" for "measure."

Figure 5.1 corresponds roughly to an "equation of value" developed by the Russian economist Dimitriev in the 1920s, i.e.,

$$V_a = N_a + \frac{1}{m_1} x_1 + \frac{1}{m_2} x_2 + \frac{1}{m_3} x_3 \dots\dots\dots\dots\dots\dots\dots + \frac{1}{m_n} x_n$$

where N_a = direct labor costs, corresponding to the block of elements denoted by b on surface B.

$\frac{1}{m_1}$ denotes the fraction attributable to labor costs in the capital

components x_1 of V_a , e.g., the block of elements c on surface C which is one of the ancestors of b_1 on surface B;

$\frac{1}{m_2}$ denotes the fraction attributable to labor costs in the capital

component x_2 used to produce x_1 . . . . etc.

The correspondence between Figure 5.1 and Dimitriev's equation of "value" is rough because Dimitriev was, in the heat of Marxist polemics no doubt, only willing to consider the role of labor in contributing to the value (somehow stored up ad infinitum) of capital. That yesterday's capital could obviously have contributed to the value and quality of today's la- bor was somehow neglected. Yet it is impossible to get rid of capital even in a format that was obviously intended to demonstrate that all the value and virtue of capital could really be attributed to its historic (and somehow stored-up) labor content. Nevertheless, Dimitriev demonstrated via what mathematicians might consider a trivial statement that all value could be reduced to a single factor . . . labor—especially if capital was left undefined, unclassified, and *made* homogeneous in some unexplained sense. In this, he was as one with many (but not all) neoclassical practitioners who expressed the opinion that economic theory would somehow be much more comfortable if all factors of production could somehow be reduced to a single factor. What then, makes capital in its real, physical presence somehow ineradicable, invaluable, and always compelling? In terms of this exposition—because of its indispensable role in the economic process—whether it is "embodied" in certain classes or vintages of "machinery," or discloses itself as "human capital" or as "smart money" or "capital ideas," capital has an ability to be an "enabler" of what was learned and done in the past to become economically viable in the present "membrane" of T (i.e., not only is "capital is what capital does"; it *is* capital because it "can do" today; it *is* what has survived as "useful" after all physical artifacts and labor content from the past are no longer relevant to "value" in the present). Capital, then, is a deeply time-specific entity. It *becomes* capital only *at that time* and if it is of value as something that *enables* labor, not because of some ethereal presence of stored up labor value from a forgotten past. In this sense, capital fulfills an indispensable role, as the principal cognitive carrier through technological time of what has been found to be permanently useful in collective economic experience (see Figure 3.2 and supporting text). Capital, then, ought not to be cast in the role of "villain" as opposed to a frequently romanticized view of labor as the antithesis of capital—with historically catastrophic repercussions. Capital is no less virtuous than labor. Nor is it any more guilty at its worst than misguided labors.

The "measurement" of the capital/output ratio (or capital co-efficient, or as an indicator of the "period of production") and plotting the course of its trend through time, has been a constant pre-occupation of economic analysis for most of the last century. Its role in the creation of business cycles, and its potential for collision with the savings-to-income ratio have often been at the center of these pre-occupations, and rightly so.

In a Telos-Technos nexus, which accepts the interactive, heterogeneous nature *and* operational reality of "capital," changes in the numerator of the ratio must be (painfully or enjoyably) traced directly to the class of capital most affected by the era of ϒ within which the changes occurred. For example, if we refer back to the table in Chapter Three of Black Box Technologies and examine the very first entry, "Super-Conductive Material," we see under the "Direction of Cost Savings" that its impact would be felt most heavily on those classes of capital invested in by government and industry that have been traditionally depended upon to generate, through the multiplier effect, the greatest possible job creation and income at low points in the business cycle. In terms of the material in Chapter Four, this would tend to compress the natural participation rate as well as eliminate the "multiplier power" that would have been available if that particular component in the flow of ϒ had never happened.

The only hope left for absorbing the enormous capacity for production that had been left unemployed from then negative ripple effects of this "ideal technology" would have to come from the income and real price effects associated with Category 2 of the CCSL and Sector 2 of omega. In accordance with the material in Chapter Two and both Ricardo's and Mill's *initial* analysis of the effects of the "machinery question" on the "interests of the working classes," this would not necessarily be "automatic compensation" or a "fundamental optimism about the ability of th economy to re-absorb labor" (Chapter 3, Appendix 4). In Chapter Six, Mill's policy recommendations on the "machinery question"—which seem to flow more from his initial analysis of the subject rather than his later accommodation to the "law of automatic compensation"—will be reviewed.

Since the time of Malthus's remarkable insights into the potentially debilitating effects of excess saving, which are frequently considered to be the direct ancestor of Keynesian attitudes toward the subject (e.g., the "paradox of thrift"), it has been recognized that the behavioral motivations to save have a profoundly different rationale than the motivations to investment and consumption.

Indeed, the basic discordance between the two, which is unnatural and inexplicable in a pure Say's law/Walrasian economy (which is equivalent to an equally pure Schumpeterian circular flow state), leads to a perpetual "out of step" dance between the savings/income ratio and the capital/output ratio, that has been the stuff of grandiose theorizing for more than a century. The gist of much of this body of (essentially business cycle) theory is a classic illustration of Veblen's warning that volatility in economic events often owes more to the behavior of those who are "disturbed" by economic stimuli, than the stimuli themselves, i.e., a case of the disturbed often becoming more disturbing to the course of events than the disturbance which confronted them, and a clear illustration of Veblen's propensity to never discount the intrusion of the irrational into the "conscious life" from which economic behavior ought never to be isolated. In this regard, we should bear in mind Ludwig Edler Mises' admonition that the word "irrational," especially when applied to (teleological) ends, can never mean the same thing to all (wo)men. A very brief review of the most relevant of such theories indicates clearly that a Telos-Technos nexus is far more comfortable with this line of thought than equilibrium based thinking. (Refer to Friedrich A. Hayek, *The Sensory Order and Limitation of Knowledge* and *Economics and Knowledge*, 1937)

In short, given that Technological time "flows" and that the "law of automatic compensation" is baseless under an initial condition equivalent to endogenizing technical change—the savings/income ratio and the capital-output ratio are in an asymmetrical relationship.

It can be accepted on the basis of several decades of growth and development theory that different savings-to-income ratios are appropriate to correspondingly different stages of economic development . . . and that in the earlier stages of economic development, the "forced savings hypothesis" often becomes painful historic reality, whether imposed from the top down as in the first "five year plans" of Stalin's U.S.S.R. or as the power of the first great "captains of industry" to impose the rule of lowest possible wage rates on their as yet unorganized labor forces, during the early years of the Industrial Revolution. Nevertheless, the standard of living of all classes of society rose indisputably during this period, no matter how perceived or reckoned.

Thus savings can be a virtue in some stages of development but not in others. Accordingly, it is worth investigating the existence of a "natural capital-to-output ratio" which varies with technological time, and from which the savings-to-income ratio should not diverge too excessively; consequently, capital in all its real heterogeneous forms becomes less scarce (tends to be a "free good") if the flow of Technological time is positive, while the potential savings pool tends to increase faster and asymmetrically. There are no assumptions here of "unlimited investment opportunities" which are symmetrical with the "law of automatic compensation"—this will be discussed in Chapter Six as the pseudo-dynamized analogue of the Say's Law–Stationary CCSL symmetry (or the "insatiability of consumers' wants"). From the time of Malthus, the doctrine of the detrimental effects of excess saving escalated from that of a periodic leakage out of the income stream, to that of a chronic tendency to hemorrhage, as a loss of multiplier power (Keynes). But in the hands of the heirs to the Austrian School, the disparity between the two escalated into the major contributor to instability in the business cycle.

The culmination of this line of thought was Hayek's over-investment hypothesis, more a description of the course of a typical business cycle than an explanation. Nevertheless, whether more historical description than explanation, or explanation by way of historical exposition, Hayek's vivid theorizing is far more compatible with the Telos-Technos process than any equilibrium based explanation . . . which may not even be possible within a mindset that insists on the presumption of "path independence" and the anti-historical posturing of the equilibrium paradigm.

At its core, Hayek's over-investment thesis rests not only on firm historical foundations but on equally solid behavioral ones. When the CCSL is not moving in phase with the process improvement component of $\mathfrak{X}$ (perfectly normal hysteresis loaded behavior, Chapter Two) then the propensity to invest takes the lead for two essentially behavioral reasons.

1. There is a tendency among investors, especially institutional ones, including banks and other lenders, to over-invest in the old familiar elements of the infrastructure, e.g., commercial and residential real estate, energy projects, etc., with a corresponding flurry of activity in the financial service industries and the money markets associated with them (e.g., the cycles of "boom and bust" in the 19th century railway building).

2. Teleologically fueled anticipations about particular elements of Category 2 of the CCSL (see relationships 1-6, Chapter Two), coupled with a "bandwagon" syndrome may also cause "animal spirits" to get the better of rational market research.

The net effect of these interactions often amounts to a kind of surrogate inflation of assets of existing companies and those who are judged to be growth loci, while simultaneously inflationary forces in the consumption sectors of the economy may be quite modest. In effect existing assets (including land) become surrogate absorbers of inflation; in place of the conventional inflation of the prices of commodities which are no longer produced with the same pain of "waiting" *or prolonged* "periods of production" (Appendix 7).

As an exercise in comparative Economic history the reader should revisit again a favorite haunt of those who revel in the history of money and "specie"—especially those who think that money "ought to be" a "neutral" enabler of exchange only . . . Walrasians, ultra-Montane indeed! Does the "surrogate" inflation of assets (on the world financial markets) arising from the sanctuary-motivated transfer of "oil money" from their "failed-nation state" sources, correspond to the hyper-inflation in Europe that followed the inflow of gold and silver "bullion" from the "Spanish" Americas during the sixteenth century?

These reasons, which are rooted in the Telos-Technos nexus are obviously not the only ones that influence asset inflation and gross overvaluation in particular capital markets. Judgements, well-founded or otherwise, about the relative stability and trustworthiness of different societies are notorious for influencing the comings and goings and even the "sanctuary" choices of capital. But the basic forces which foster such surrogate asset inflation are omni-present and are the primal underlying causes of business cycles. These cannot be adequately explained in a framework which leaves technology exogenous; indeed their very existence cannot be accounted for, because economically viable technological development is now the dominant form of Schumpeter's classic statement of the primary causes of economic development.

Radical changes in Telos can annihilate capital value. When such cycles of over-investment peak, the particular classes of capital which enjoyed the most exaggerated inflation of their values frequently glut the markets for years afterwards. This applies as well to the "human capital" factors associated with particular markets; for example, the various aviation and aircraft industries with their highly skilled and educated labor forces, which absorbed many years and dollars of heavy investment, find themselves obliged to seek jobs in other industries where their accumulated skills and experience are of little direct value. An exaggerated example of this were the great demobilizations following the wars of the twentieth century, wherein the highly specialized and demanding skills as well as the very expensive embodied capital that constituted the tools of their trade, became virtually worthless to the people and society that they once served as a matter of life or death. The spectacular growth of the machine tool industries and the standardization of work procedures associated with mass production from the mid-nineteenth century to the present time wiped out entire trades and professions that had been traditionally respected for centuries . . . not just stages of production within related industries and trades. The phenomenon known as "de-skilling" is simply a continuation of this trend. For example, the assembly of electrical and electronic components into appliances and electronic products can often be carried out by semi-literate workers with very little investment in training, by a visual-spatial procedure that simply fits the components onto a surface containing the outline of their shapes; no "apprenticeship," no "breaking in" time, but a de facto return to the days of "hire-purchase," not much different than the conditions of field agriculture.

Between roughly 1898 and 1909 the great Thorstein Veblen wrote a prescient series of articles about, among other equally important topics, the nature and quantifiability of capital—i.e., *Quarterly Journal of Economics*, *Journal of Political Economy*, *American Economic Association— Series 3*. For purposes of this chapter, we urge our readers to review Veblen's admonitions to distinguish between "the aggregate of industrial capital" as merely a subjectively valued "pecuniary" quantity (appropriately indexed basis, *"functionally considered."* Veblen believed that to depend on "pecuniary" quantification, however manipulated statistically, was to invite a chain of highly misleading conclusions, because "pecuniary" valuation only of capital was, in our terms, spurious quantifiability incarnated. I.e., "The disparity between industrial and pecuniary capital is something much more than just a matter of an arbitrarily chosen point of view: just as the difference between the pecuniary and industrial employments, which are occupied with one or another *category* (class) of capital, mean something more than the same thing under different aspects." There we have it! Beware of treating differences in kind, (which are equivalent to distinctive qualitative differences—heterogeneity) as if they are homogeneous technical units, expressed as "coin of the realm" *and* stress "consider function" or as the late Joan Robinson put it "capital is as capital does." What would Veblen have thought of the concept of "total factor productivity" (TFP) and its weird metamorphoses into the "Solow Residual"? If the reader needs further enlightenment as to which side of "the pond" really won the "Cambridge capital controversy" (hands down!), please consult the May 1970 issue of the *Canadian Journal of Economics*—"capital theory up to date" or alternatively: *Gulliver's Travels* by Jonathan Swift regarding the professors of the Grand Academy of Lagado—or Frederick V. Hayek himself on the heterogeneity of capital. All these phenomena have been described by Joseph Schumpeter as "creative destruction" after the role model of Shiva, the Hindu lord of destruction, among others.

Once again the principle of the creative destruction of capital is more obvious in a military context than in a traditional economic framework, although war *is* an economic activity in the context of Sector 2 of omega. For example, the ultimate annihilation of capital value in a military context is via nuclear weapons. In this respect the Enola Gay eliminated the need for an entire fleet of B-29s which would have been required to annihilate the same quantity of "fixed" and "human" capital, using conventional ordinance . . . a rather morbid example, but one quoted by Robert Oppenheimer from the Bhagavad Gita at Los Alamos in July 1945. A much more restrained example of the principle of creative destruction is that performed by Kali, the irresistible power of transcendent time, which is a much better fit with the concept of obsolescence, a vital component of the manifold nature of technological time. In this context, the principle of obsolescence may also subsume the notion of capital saving, by considering it as the transformation that is effected by the $\mathcal{T}$ on particular classes of capital. For example, the effect of portable computer systems, essentially transferable office locations, on the permanent ratio of commercial real estate to all forms of fixed capital, would be an intriguing prognosis that could be developed from a Telos-Technos approach.

It would appear that capital is the economic variable most vulnerable to the principle of creative destruction. But this process is operationally meaningless within the context of "homogeneous" capital, which purports to be more "scientific" because it "quantifies." To condense the argument, Taxonomic discipline combined with the concept of technological time, is the only procedure that would turn Schumpeter's philosophic principle into an authentic operational tool of analysis. It would also belatedly recognize Veblen's unjustly ignored warnings about the consequences of the slipshod use of "pecuniary valuations" of capital. The cases of Solow, Jorgenson, and Grilliches and their chain of heirs are a bleak testimony to the prescient nature of Veblen's teachings on that subject.

Appendix 1

In *Das Kapital*, Volume III, Chapter 4, Frederick Engels, in his capacity as a business man no doubt, makes the following intriguing observations—about the "release" of working capital by outside progress in transportation and communication infrastructures, which had . . . "in the last fifty years doubled or trebled . . . the productive capacity of the *capital*" engaged in the world commerce; and . . . improved efficiency of the fixed capital of industry as in "the recently discovered methods of making iron and steel, such as the processes of Bessemer, Siemens, Gilchrist-Thomas, ..." Was Engels a precursor of Solow?

Appendix 2

An obviously unintentional precursor of the hyper-embodiment thesis was the science fiction classic "*Metropolis*" filmed in 1925 by Fritz Lang, serving here in the role of an economic parable. In *Metropolis*, *all* technical advance is embodied in a great volume and bulk of machinery, which is simply made congruent with *all* capital. Labor is faceless, uniform and "homogeneous"; it simply "tends" the productive capital which is mostly underground. The labor has no choices in even the most basic elements of its consumption and living standards; it does not even have the right to live and work on the surface. Only the controllers of this voluminous capital have the right to enjoy a life style on the surface. This whole order is eventually threatened by the invention of a "humanoid" robot that will presumably replace even the homogeneous labor . . . perhaps the last word in "embodiment" of *total* factor costs of production, i.e., machines will tend machines. The dilemma is not resolved by economic theory.

Appendix 3

One of the most celebrated cases of the *political* economy of conflict—i.e., using monetary values as a "veil" for different interpretations of the same events in economic (and military) history relates to the valuation of eleven billion United States dollars placed on the "lend-lease" aid provided to the former U.S.S.R. during the 1941-1945 period. The spokesmen and propagandists for that unhappy regime, especially during the immediate post-war period, continually denigrated this figure as being only a fraction of the value of the war matériel that the former Soviet Union had provided to its armed forces, not to mention the unparalled human sacrifices that were demanded in the most terrible campaign in the history of war. The Americans were quite understandably embittered by what appeared to be a position of ingratitude toward them, when in fact they had done their very best for the Soviet ally under very difficult circumstances and, as was subsequently proven, very effectively.

But when the smoke and mirrors of the post-Stalinist period had finally been cleared away, an exact classification of the matériel provided told quite a different story than a bare-bones description of "$11 billion." Virtually all of the aid—the military capital of war—came in the form of matériel that the Soviets were unable to produce for themselves up to the required quantity and standards. For example, more than one million miles of almost "leak-proof" field-telephone cable, tens of thousands of well-made, mass-produced radio and wireless sets for the Soviet Air force, their tanks, and signal corps; fields of activity in which the Soviets were notoriously deficient, even for decades after the war; not to mention nearly half a million land vehicles of all types, enough food-rations to provide, on average, at least one high protein meal a day for their fighting men and women . . . and much, much more. Even the Germans commented sourly on the impact of the Red Army's vastly improved mobility from the huge fleets of Dodge, Studebaker, and Ford trucks. Once again, the polar extreme of war (Sector 2 of omega) has clarified a point that applies to all economic activity classified under the rubric of capital.

Appendix 4

The fine art of inappropriately homogenizing capital so as to tame it for usage in the more convoluted defenses of the neoclassical position has been mentioned earlier in this chapter. In practice, such arguments usually employ the techniques of capitalizing or discounting in the general direction of a pre-arranged result, in a more or less circular way, choosing a "well cooked" rate of interest or profit. This is certainly as good a way as any of avoiding the insistent operational heterogeneity of capital, by confounding the traditional arithmetic for describing the efficiency of *investment,* with the *structural classification of the capital that investment buys.*

Appendix 5

One of the earliest attempts to "quantify" the human capital factor in a more or less taxonomic way, in order to predict and compare performance levels, occurred in the context of very basic military intelligence during World War I. At that time the Imperial German General Staff was supplied with the following numbers which, as it turned out, did co-relate rather well with small unit performance of the two armies, *in that war* . . . during that particular "cut" in T.

Average Number of Non Commissioned Officers per Infantry Company	Imperial Germany 12	Russian Empire 2

or for a much earlier example

It was noted by officers of the day, by the middle of the sixteenth century, that in the previous centuries it had often taken years to train an effective long-bowman; but it was only a matter of months or even weeks to train a musketeer on a cranky and unreliable match-lock weapon (on a heavy mounting) to fire significantly *fewer* shots per minute, over a much shorter trajectory, than the long-bowman. Yet the musketeer prevailed and evolved in to the rifle-man. Is this the first example (after wineries) of the Austrian notion of the "period of production" or of "waiting" for the maturation of human capital and the trade-offs it engenders? Even at the earliest stages of a technology . . . and an "ideal" one at that? (See Chapter Three.)

Appendix 6

The manifold nature of technological time also includes the role of the Hindu goddess, Mother Kali, who symbolizes the irresistible power of transcendent time. In this respect, the principle of "creative destruction" applied to the history of economic development by Joseph Schumpeter, (after Shiva) may be an accelerated version of the "Kalic" principle.

Appendix 7

The great Japanese asset inflation of the late 1980s and early '90s remains a classic if grotesque example of the phenomenon of hyper inflation of asset values; indeed, it is the epitome of capital playing the role of surrogate absorber of inflation, especially in the local real estate and utilities markets. This recent example in Japan's economic history is hardly unrelated to Japan's legendary reputation for high propensities to save, undaunted by a traditional acceptance of unusually low rates of return on investment by Western standards. It will be interesting to see whether these post-war modes of Japanese economic behavior will continue in the face of a rapidly declining capital/output ratio, no matter how this is "measured" or defined.

Chapter Six

A Summing Up: Implications for Further Consideration

What position has a Telos-Technos nexus assumed with respect to earlier points of view that are familiar to the reader? In order to answer this question we must return to the ultimate *benchmark* of economic thought known as "Say's Law of Markets." It has served as a convenient punching bag for an interesting assortment of economists and economic thinkers for more than seven generations. Yet it remains unassailable *as stated* and unchallengeable within the domain of its natural boundary conditions. These may be stated simply as perfect competition and smoothly automatic price regulation—and Technos is constant. Thus it is also analytically equivalent to Schumpeter's description of a pure "circular flow" economy, one in which development, particularly of the technical kind, is absent. There is really not very much that can be deduced from the conditions of Schumpeter's pure "circular flow" that cannot be similarly drawn out of Say's law *as stated*. Schumpeter set up his pure "circular flow" economy as a point of *departure* from which, as he makes clear, one *cannot* deduce the principles of development; new conditions must be introduced. Interestingly enough, Schumpeter does not mention Say's law, as such, in Chapter One of the *Theory of Economic Development*, but does acknowledge the "method due to *Leon Walras*" as the source of his "well known device" of holding "*technical knowledge*, tastes, culture . . . the *same*"—in a footnote.

The attributes of a perfect *Say/Walras* economy and Schumpeter's pure *Circular Flow* economy may be very generally summarized below and are almost identical with Ludwig V. Mises "analytical foil," *The Evenly Rotating Economy* (ERE),

1. Very little uncertainty to no uncertainty, and perfect competition.
2. Technology is constant, either because it is exogenous in the Say/Walras case, or rigorously stated as a boundary condition as in Schumpeter's.
3. Money is a "veil" of real repetitive transactions, which is tacked on as another commodity and neutrally cleared by its own *interest as the price of money* self-regulating mechanism (Walras) or the price of money is zero, as in no interest rate (Schumpeter).
4. Consumption patterns and tastes are constant or, in our terms, only Category *1* of the Current Conception of the Standard of Life exists. In Say's case they were described as "insatiable," but this cannot be interpreted in the 20th century mass consumption sense. It really conveys a sense of up to a fixed habitual standard of living as in Category 1 of the CCSL.
5. There are no business cycles in the Schumpeterian case. In the Say/Walras case they are stable and predictable with periods short and amplitudes *almost* flat. In his original formulation, J.B. Say allowed for small deviations of under- or over-production by sellers, which were swiftly re-adjusted to market conditions by a smoothly automatic regulator . . . a laissez faire price system.

The only "fly in the ointment" of the "impossibility of general glut" axiom was the intrusive reality of their occurrence "since time immemorial." Indeed, even J.M. Keynes experienced this dilemma and felt the need to reject some of the classical explanations (the "spillover effect") offered to explain the "Paradox." Indeed, Keynes stressed that *his* Marshallian" "short-run" approach started with aggregate income and output "given." Disequilibriums between supply and demand at the inter sectoral level (the two-digit S.I.C. code level) could only explain internal shifts (micro). Such "plus-minus" spillovers could not "add-up" to (gestalt-like change?) in the aggregate "whole"—especially when clinging to the original. Say/Walras boundary conditions: (1)"tastes" are given (2) state of industrial "Technos" is given.

In a famous quotation (1926), he gave voice to his frustration:

"We are faced at every turn with the problem of organic unity of discreteness, of discontinuity; the whole is not equal to the sum of the parts, comparisons of quantity fail us; small changes produce large effects; the assumptions of a uniform and homogeneous continuum are not satisfied."

— and *all that in 1926!*

or

"A static, equilibrium system can never be used to explain business cycles."

—Adolph Löwe,
one of Hayek's colleagues.

and

"Those who wish to solve the business cycle problem, must sacrifice the static system."

—Ludwig Lachmann

or

Why going from "micro" to "macro" is not obvious.

Was the "spill-over" effect, offered by some classical economists, (Robert Torrens, James Mill, etc.) as an explanation for business cycles and all their accompanying "ills" (involuntary unemployment, business failures, idle capital, etc., in spite of the purported "impossibility of general glut," simply an early "Ptolemaic" attempt to circumvent the gestalt nature of interactive, not aggregative, economic events? It has reappeared constantly ever since in poorly disguised form, often with a surfeit of mathematically portly accompaniment; as "models"—giving rise to even more heated and convoluted argument than even the classical economists could endure.

In squeezing out even the mild hysteresis of the classical economists ("the hesitation of things" as defined by Ernst Mach), all of whom allowed for periods of adjustments in even the most "determined" human economic responses (especially Jean Baptist Say, McCulloch and Mill (J.S.), the neo"classical" school abandoned itself to a requirement for the timelessly (and hopelessly?) "Ergodic." This fatal neglect of the meaning and *function* of *real time* in human response and relations was . . . driven by the simultaneously determined solutions to the aggregate exchange matrix, demanded by the Walrasian "tatonnement" paradigm.

This in turn "morphed" into the notoriously time-annihilating "neoclassical" paradigm, the very embodiment of Alfred Marshall's insight that questions about how to deal with time lie at the root of almost every unresolved problem in our subject. For further elaboration of this fatal flaw in the neoclassical paradigm, the reader should consult Amartya Sen's distinction between "determined solutions" as defined by mathematicians and "determinism" as viewed in the "real" world of "cause and effect" . . . a man who understands quite a bit about both sides of that coin . . . to say the least.

The Say/Walras system evolved into the Neoclassical version:

1. Technology is held as exogenous.
2. Consumers are insatiable, as in Scitovsky (see Chapter Two, Appendix 2 and Chapter Three, Appendix 4).
3. Investment opportunities confronting would-be investors are "unlimited" in Hayek's sense of the term.
4. There is an underlying (or subliminal) assumption of "automatic compensation" as the natural reaction of consumer markets (see Chapter Three, Appendix 4 again).
5. Business cycles exist but they are not caused by any inherent lack of will in consumers or investors but by accumulations of rigidities such as the "stickiness of wages and prices," "asymmetric information," etc.; i.e., in the neoclassical mode, they are difficult to explain, other than as the consequences of deviant behavior.
6. Money is "neutral" in its "long run "behavior.
7. Growth is normal, natural, and essentially stabilizing and beneficial in the long run. There is no inherent conflict between growth and environmental considerations, because growth is congruent with development.
8. All economic phenomena can be expressed in terms of the Equilibrium paradigm.
9. The "passenger pigeon" scenario is deemed to be trivial in the "long run," another way of stating that technology as a "free good" will behave as a "cargo cult" rescuer from any of the consequences of the passenger pigeon scenario "in the long run."

The Keynesian system is seen as a "halfway house" in terms of the Telos-Technos nexus, a doorway to a far less "determined" *future* than its predecessors could allow for, and one which needed "help" to arrive in reasonably acceptable condition—*in the short run*. Its broad outlines are described below.

1. Technology is still held exogenous.
2. Uncertainty is endemic to the functioning of the system; indeed it is inherent in the behavior of economic man, whether as investor, saver, or consumer.
3. Say's law is not operational.
4. Investment and Savings behavior are asymmetrical and arise from different motivations in economic man.
5. Business cycles are probable and capable of becoming long and deep. Secular stagnation and long term glut are inherent in the system because of these asymmetries in economic behavior.
6. Money is *not* neutral; it affects economic behavior and has consequences. Consider the following comments made by Keynes in his delivery of the Galton Lecture to the Eugenics Society in 1937:

"There is a chronic tendency *throughout human history* for the propensity to save to be stronger than the inducement to invest."

and

"It is doubtful whether average levels of *consumption* will rise sufficiently to require the amounts of investment necessary to support full employment under existing social relationships."

An even more prescient comment was made by Knut Wicksell *in 1924.*

"It is difficult to escape the conclusion that there *must* be a certain lack of harmony . . . the difference between technical progress and human wants causes a jerkiness in the organism and the jerks are transformed into a wave proceeding in a certain rhythm, because of the structure of human society itself."

It would appear from the above quotes that Keynes did not believe in the "insatiability" of human wants, whereas Wicksell before him did not believe in their ability to react in phase with technical progress in the ability to satisfy more of them. It is also probable from the quotation that, in addition to the traditional Keynesian motives to save, Keynes, at the very least, suspected one more which could be laid at the feet of consumers: namely that a significant percentage of unnecessary saving could be blamed on the reactions of the consumption accumulation process in not keeping pace with the opportunities to consume more; this "motivation" to save could be a case of saving not by intent but by *consumers default*. Wicksell's comment, in terms of this exposition, is a direct allusion to the phenomenon of hysteresis as being a built-in component of all human economic behavior, a sort of backhand acknowledgment that the *normal* decision-making process of consumers at the "threshold of consumption" in response to perceptions of Category 2 of the CCSL, is *not* knee jerk at all (see Chapter Two). Arguably, Wicksell was rejecting "in his heart" the subliminal assumption of the "law" of automatic compensation. The implications of this observation also point in the direction of "technical progress" being a primary and omnipresent agent of uncertainty, as it is, in a Telos-Technos nexus; and as such, not a mysteriously deviant and unjustified result of errant human behavior.

It was upon this stake that Keynes impaled himself, in the eyes of his many critics; after all, he understood in his bones that a mature economy ("throughout history" is a rather strong version) was *empirically* contingency loaded. But he laid much of the blame on the uncertainty of investors' "expectations" as the principle agent of all uncertainty. But Keynes explicitly (in Chapter 18 of the "General Theory . . .") held *technos constant* and "tastes" as well. With such boundary conditions, Say's law cannot be disproved; therefore there is no basic underlying reason why "investors' expectations" should be such a strong agent of uncertainty, or should even vary significantly from one time to the next; thus he was accused of failing to disprove the operation of Say's law (by not explicitly denying its underlying foundations of "insatiability") on the one hand, while affirming the logical consequences of its non-operation (i.e., uncertainty) with the other. In this respect Keynes was in conflict with Schumpeter's consistency, not complementary with it. After all, Schumpeter was on solid ground by stating that interest rates are zero, in the presence of the no-risk, no uncertainty environment provided by the absence of development, especially of its most important manifestation—

technical. Schumpeter's zero-interest rate hypothesis is arguably the first occasion to explicitly link a class of monetary events, i.e., interest rates, with a state of real economic events; i.e., development, or the lack of it. In our terms he causally linked a no-flow state of Technological time with an interest rate number. It's not just wishful thinking about a hoped-for one-to-one correspondence between one chosen variable and another . . . say some chosen proxy for technological "progress" co-related with another chosen monetary variable. While such criticism is logically justified, as far as it goes, it fails to take account of Keynes's intellectual and historical milieu. In his deep concern with the "short run," the clear and present crisis of the 1930s that had to be addressed immediately, Keynes was seeking to justify a "quick fix," the need for which could not even be acknowledged by the economic orthodoxy of his day. As for considerations of technical change as the principal root of uncertainty that undermined the empirical validity of Say's law, it clearly lay outside the "Scope and Methodology of Political Economy"—that is, it was "exogenous" to the subject according to John Nivelle Keynes; this rule was honored more in the breach than in the observance by his son.

But in so doing, Keynes was underscoring his oft-repeated comment that Economics was more of a "moral science" than a "natural" one (see Appendix 3). In this he was certainly at one with Adam Smith, and much more in the British tradition of Political Economy than the French one, as typified by Walras. At a more practical level, Keynes understood clearly, in terms of his own experience, that the placement of capital was becoming a riskier and riskier proposition, as the need for it became more and more unpredictable. In the end, Keynes simply reached *his* inevitable conclusion that the capitalist system in its natural state (as defined by inherent uncertainty) needed a conservateur—booster shots, so to speak, outside the multiplier of the private sector, applied to Sector 2 of omega, in terms of Telos-Technos. This was, more or less, what was taking place in Germany, the United States and, for quite different reasons, the former U.S.S.R. at the time, each in their own way, of course. An even more vigorous boost toward full employment "equilibrium" was imminent, via *Sector* 2 of the operation Telos' of their societies (see Appendix 1).

A major misunderstanding about the importance that Keynes attached to the power of debt is currently in vogue among certain so-called Neo-Keynesians and post-Keynesians. For example, the most socialistic of the Neo-Keynesians advocate that there is a basic trade-off between the benefits of high levels of expenditure on "social programs" and a firm policy of arresting the accumulation of public debt through elimination of annual budgetary deficits. From their point of view the accumulation of public debt is a small price to pay for the deep social benefits and the "keeping the lid on" function of such spending. At no time did Keynes ever advocate the virtual sidetracking of monetary and debt considerations by government to the extent that his contemporary acolytes claim. Indeed in both international and internal debt management, Keynes was wisely and presciently aware of just how poisonous and conflict-engendering power relationships rooted in debt could get. From *Economic Consequences of the Peace* (1919) through a *Treatise on Money* (1930) to his prominent role in setting up the World Bank and the International Monetary Fund (*Bretton Woods*, 1944) plus a non stop itinerary of public pronouncements and articles, Keynes never underestimated the lethal effects that debt relationships could have on international relationships and social stability when they were politically abused.

At times, the more extreme of the nouveau Keynesians seem to advocate that the generation of internal debt is nothing more than a "neutral" sleight of hand, no more harmful than a book-keeping protocol, but at the super-macro level. In the real world (i.e., at the level of the firm and the individual) such book-keeping protocols have a habit of becoming too creative, and their consequences something more than neutral. Why then should their aggregated consequences add up to harmless neutrality at the level of macro-economic policy? And do their consequences never interact with the economies of other jurisdictions? In the light of Telos-Technos, this kind of thinking is not only an abuse of the principle of contra-cyclical budgeting when debt loads are already formidable; it also reveals a stunning lack of awareness of the extent to which economic policy and the countless number of micro-relationships underlying it interact in a *gestalt* relationship, rather than one which can be satisfactorily "measured" to an exact aggregation. In gestalt relationships in other social sciences, many practitioners consider themselves fortunate to forecast even the general direction of the consequences of their stimuli . . . and in much less complex systems than the macro-economic. And it is notoriously true that the more complex systems are, the more likely they will respond to well-intentioned manipulations according to the "law" of unintended consequences; this "law" has dominated more of economic history than all the others combined. After all, is any system more complex than one which involves an almost infinite universe of human interaction and conflicting motivations?

Say's "Law" and the Monetarist Conceit

A Say/Walras economy is in principle highly amenable to "fine tuning" and a console-control-programming approach, provided the programmer knows which buttons to press and when. In this respect the controller of the console is like a super-perfect choreographer who pre-determines every future position of a vast, almost uncountable number of interactive dancers, by a *nearly* automatic system of commands that corrects any combination of deviant movements by and number of the dancers. In this way the great dance always seems perfectly co-ordinated and harmonious to an onlooker. Only the great choreographer knows how close to a chaotic comic jumble of frenetic motion it can all become, if even the slightest deviation from the program by one dancer is allowed to interact with any of the other performers for more than a split second.

The command console consists entirely of buttons connected to those parameters wired to the monetary system, interest rates, and the great financial institutions. Through these highly trained "dancers" and them alone, the great aggregates of the economic system will be manipulated from one equilibrium state to a higher one, along stable, minimally perturbed growth paths. For these reasons alone, static equilibrium theory continues to remain a comfort to policy enforcers because it creates the illusion that the economy can be held still long enough to control it by well-choreographed monetary manipulations. A cruder analogy is to summon up the image of the tail of a Chihuahua dog that has been grafted on to the rump of a St. Bernard. If properly manipulated, the tail can somehow wag the great dog. The great risk of the monetarist conceit is that the great "choreographer" is still himself part of the choreography, as the receiver and interpreter of feedback from the dancers—and just as prone to erroneous reaction as they are. In the same way, the tail of the Chihuahua dog is also part of the great body it must wag. To paraphrase Veblen, at what point will the reaction of the manipulators become more disturbing than the disturbances they are trying to control?

By extension of this analogy can these great interacting economic aggregates be controlled by a console routine that links control of unemployment rates to rates of inflation *controllable from the* interest rate "buttons"? Will the dancers called inflation and unemployment always dance in perfect harmony? What if the wrong buttons are pushed . . . harder and more frequently as the feedback received deviates more and more from the pre-determined choreography?

In an environment where asset inflation is just as probable as the traditional commodity inflation, the Phillips curve (with its implicit assumption that commodity inflation/unemployment is the dominant trade-off for policy-making purposes) becomes somewhat dubious. It is not deniable that under certain conditions bordering on the cataclysmic, which are not impossible, a general and serious commodity inflation can occur. This will be discussed in the last section of the chapter. But in a Telos-Technos description of the *economic process*, the most important trade-off that must be managed is between the natural participation rate and employment levels on the one hand and contingency-loaded variations in the CCSL and omega on the other (see Chapter Four).

In a typical heuristic program for allocating scarce factors of production to obtain certain economic objectives, technology is held constant as expressed by fixed technical coefficients of homogeneously quantifiable factor inputs—usually labor and some form of capital or inventory. In such models there exists a category of inputs called "free goods." The technical conditions of a free good are:

1. The input of the commodity/factor of production cannot exceed its output on the previous period.
2. However, if the input is less than the output, the factor of production is described as a free good.

—D.G. Champernowne, 1945, "A Note on John von Neumann's Article" *Review of Economic Studies,* 13, 10-18, as quoted by R.G.D. Allen in *Mathematical Economics*, 1963 Edition, Macmillan and Co. LTD.

Combining the above definition with the material from Chapter Four produces the following conclusion:

A positive flow of Technological time (not a guaranteed future by any means), *in itself, tends to* make particular classes of capital and labor a free good, at a rate that varies with its flow . . . the nitty-gritty of changes in *kind.* The only countervailing forces that oppose this tendency are the CCSL and Sector 2 of omega. Since this description of the economic process cannot be usefully modeled by employing tautological relationships (such as the Say/Walras identity) as a benchmark, the general purpose of economic policy in this context is to provide a kind of multi-faceted gyroscope that stabilizes the key variables which are considered most important to the maintenance of reasonable (not guaranteed) stability and freedom of choice—while at the same time preserving the delicate balance of power between government and civil society. That is, there are no conservateurs or fiat control parameters (such as interest rates) available as policy tools that can be used with the same old confidence. The key variables, by common consensus in virtually all societies, are a fair distribution of the quantity of work required among the available sectors of the labor force (= resultant level of employment);

and

preventing the widespread and insidious formation of degenerate income levels that cannot sustain, at the very least, some minimal level of comfort in terms of Category 1 of the CCSL. Von Neumann's definition of a "free good" can be quite revealing if it is applied to an era of ꝯ characterized by declining Natural participation rates. When the amount of labor embodying that class of human capital which was "outputed" in period t–1, is always less than what it is needed for as input, now (period 't')—then there is no "waiting" in the classical sense. Nor is there a "period of production" in the Austrian school's sense, required to accumulate that particular class of capital. Then what is the point during such an era of ꝯechnological time in pursuing "robust" immigration policies? Is this simply a case of "carrying coals to Newcastle"? . . . with a heightened probability of all manner of social unrest and needless costs to the various levels of government? The "law of unintended consequences" indeed! . . . in its most negative guise.

It is a clear consequence of the gestalt gap in the economic process that all the relentless seeking of efficiency at the micro-economic level by firms, individuals, and institutions does not necessarily "add up" to economic stability as it *ought to* if the economic process were nothing more than a steady state growth path from one level of equilibrium to another (or from one rest point in the "space of decision rules" to another).

With this insistence on recycled equilibrium theory as still the last word in economic analysis, the continuing obsession with Le Chatelier's principle (now approaching its diamond jubilee) comes as no surprise. After all, if this blatant mimicry from physical chemistry could somehow be grafted on to the multiple equilibrium construct, the neoclassical school could then explain any and all change in the position of equilibrium states as the consequence of that most exogenous of all *shock* forces (Technos, the Promethean imperative) and never have to be confronted with the problem of time–path-dependency . . . or economic history as its own special sequence of events linked by its own unique set of cause and effect.

Underlying all contemporary thinking and practice of economic policy is the notion that something close to "full employment" of a variable labor force is a goal to be achieved at *any cost* (see *Dogs and Demons: The Dark Side of Japan* by Alex Kerr). The definition of "full employment" (not to mention a certain "semantic" perplexity)* has suffered somewhat in recent years because of the continuing controversy about what constitutes the "natural unemployment rate." This is considered to be of vital importance, because if a more or less consensus of agreement could be reached on the value of this number, its complement would then be, presumably, the "natural" level of employment—the rationally arrived-at standard toward which policy initiatives should be aimed. The fatal circularity in such thinking lies in its subliminal equating of "full" to "natural," and behind it lies the neoclassical conceit of identifying anything other than full employment of all available resources as somehow unnatural compared to what is ultimately the natural outcome of a Say/Walrasian economy. All this, of course, is another outcropping of the gestalt gap that deforms so much of neoclassical analysis *combined with* a lethal dose of "Hume's Guillotine" . . . the principle that one can never deduce what *ought to be* from what is. And it is very much at odds with the material in Chapter Four, especially the implications of the natural participation rate.

And this leads us to the core misunderstanding that it is a fallacy that the "natural employment" level is congruent with "full employment." By retaining the "ought-to-be" of "Natural Level of Employment → Full Employment" and damn the nitty-gritty details, both the "libertarian"

---

* "Why Is the Unemployment Rate So High at Full Employment?" Robert E. Hall, R.A. Gordon, Charles Holt. *Brookings Papers on Economic Activity*, Vol. 1970, No. 3 (1970), pp. 369-410. "A Theory of the Natural Unemployment Rate and Duration of Employment," *Journal of Monetary Economics* Vol. 5, April, 1979.

branch of the "Austrian School" and the unreconstructed "positivists" (neo"classical" economists) are ignoring David Hume's profound and timeless admonition: "We cannot deduce what ought to be from what is." They are "assuming away," up-front, the very contingent outcomes that good economic thinking should "discover," however painfully, i.e., both "schools' have the great "gyroscope*-in-the-sky," the ultimate "laissez-faire" abuse of the venerable "invisible-hand" concept, hardwired into their minds. They have, with certain exceptions, convinced themselves that the nitty-gritty details of changes in "tastes," goals of human action, and technological time do not matter to our grand theorizing about the "big-picture." The "libertarian" branch of the Austrian school ought to know better because of the great Karl Menger's definition of "complexity" in economic life and Hayek's development of his seminal thinking.

In itself, this is a paradoxical departure from the best lessons of "methodological-individualism." Still haunted by the "hermeneutic" ghost of the great hyperinflation of the early 1920s and the great depression of the 1930s, these comparatively few but otherwise admirable voices of reason continue to insist that any and all intervention by government or wrong-headed monetary authorities—especially when combined with the fractional-reserve banking system—is the true source of all failures in maintaining more or less healthy levels of economic activity. These "gremlins" are, in effect—and possibly with the best of intentions—sending the wrong "signals" to those who make the big decisions in the market place. They are, inadvertently, interfering with the circulation of the "natural" lubricant of the great automatic "gyroscope-in the-sky"—spontaneous-order itself—and their "designs" from "above" cannot but fail to bring on the "law of unintended consequences" in its most negative manifestations. Their counterparts among the many unreconstructed "positivists" of the neoclassical "school" cling to a different version of the gyroscopic

---

*   "Gyroscopic" feedback or homeostatic feedback is feedback that leads to "self"stabilizing (equilibrating) systems *versus* feedback that leads to oscillating systems, that don't necessarily lead to stabilization → where "positive" outcomes such as full employment are episodic, not an "inevitable" state. The reader should return to Chapter Four and William Vickrey's observation of the rarity through economic history of (the Utopian state?) of full employment.

fallacy: Anything less than "full-employment," with due attention to the "natural rate of unemployment" (the last word in their frequent resort to the paradoxical world of "residual-operators" . . . e.g., Solow's assignation of technological change to this "holistic" netherworld) is a remediable deviance from that which is "natural." Here are some examples of "deviance" from the Say-Walras debouchment, with its explicit axioms of:

1. symmetrical-distribution of knowledge of productive technology and "tastes" (given—as in fixed technical co-efficients and transitive preference schedules)
2. Perfectly adequate capabilities for calculating all benefits and utilities associated with a given transaction. The deviances are listed in no particular order below.
   a. asymmetrically distributed information
   b. sticky wages
   c. co-ordination failure
   d. exogenous shocks to "natural " equilibrium states, etc.

In principle and (policy) practice, all these deviations from the natural equilibrium of economic life have remedies, which will restore the "good" and the "beneficial" → which is the "natural" state → where the general (or aggregate) economy really "tends" to go. Indeed, both versions of the "great-gyroscope-in-the-sky" seem to harbor some kind of "Polyanna" vitalism (however subliminal) built into their mindsets.

In *Principles of Political Economy*, Chapter Six, John Stuart Mill initially rejects John Ramsay McCulloch's argument that the introduction of "machinery" into a productive process will lead automatically to the re-absorption of any labor displaced . . . the so-called "law" of automatic compensation. By *machinery* Mill meant, in accordance with the usage of his time, the embodied symbol of any commercially viable technical advance to industry, as did McCulloch—not mere accumulation of a greater and greater bulk of (constant vintage) capital. Such usage of the word "machinery" as shorthand for any and all technical advances continued well into the twentieth century. A typical example of this usage is to be found in the twentieth century classic *Mechanization Takes Command* by Sigfried Giedion. Giedion was well aware that "mechanization" or "machinery" was not synonymous with any and all technological progress. But it made for convenient allegory.

Interestingly enough, Mill did not believe *initially* that the price re-ductions of commodities or real income effects for the surviving job-holding consumers, would be an efficient "conservateur" for re-absorb-ing the purchasing power of displaced workers because "demand for commodities is not (necessarily) demand for labor," as quoted in previ-ous chapters of this exposition.

However, Mill eventually espouses a very strong form of McCulloch's law; it was stronger than McCulloch's, because even under perfect com-petition, as required by J.B. Say, McCulloch allowed that the process of re-absorption could be slow in effecting the required adjustments and leave pockets of distress. However, Mill proceeded to deny that techni-cal progress (machinery) could injure the interests of the working classes *even in the short term.* Whatever Mill's ambivalence in usage ("fixed capital," "machinery") may have meant to his Victorian colleagues and to him on different occasions, Mill could never quite suppress his doubts that the "machinery" question was not quite settled.

He even fears that the initial and direct labor displacing effects of "machinery" will be re-enforced intensely by their secondary effects: that is, their tendency to encourage further economies of scale in their labor-reducing consequences and concentrating a greater and greater share of industrial and wage control power in the hands of a smaller and smaller number of capitalists. Although this foresight is incorrectly credited to Marx by his acolytes, their mentor's only "contribution" to the subject was to falsely accuse both his predecessors and his contemporaries of believing in the "naïve" version of the "harmless" effects of "machin-ery," namely that the labor displaced by the introduction of machinery would be *automatically* re-absorbed in its manufacture. Like his prede-cessor Ricardo (see Chapter Two, Appendix 6), Mill knew in his bones that the "machinery question" was not settled. Indeed, he felt this so strongly that he went further than any one else before or since and advo-cated that government should somehow encourage policies that restricted private business decisions in their introduction of labor saving "machin-ery." Superb logician that he was, Mill must have clearly understood that such a definitive policy recommendation could not possibly be in-ferred from his later accommodation to the strongest version of the "law" of automatic compensation (see Appendix 2).

Seen in this light, Norbert Wiener's prognostication, quoted in the introduction to Chapter Four, is the most extreme version of Mill's un-derlying and suppressed doubts about the "law" of automatic compensation, i.e., he predicted in our terms, an extreme lag in consumers' decision-making associated with Category 2 of the CCSL (See Chapter Two). This kind of hysteresis is perfectly natural behavior in human terms because there is no inherent reason why such processes on the part of consumers should be perfectly in phase (co-ordinated?) with augmented powers of production. To even believe that there is some kind of "co-ordination failure" here is to partake of McCulloch's "law" of automatic compensation, or deducing "what ought-to-be from what is" ("Hume's guillotine"). This is indeed a stunning contrast to the Polyanna optimism and blind faith expressed by a congress of contemporary economists nearly half a century later (see Chapter Three, Appendix 4).

What emerges clearly from such congresses is that the neoclassical mindset, which underlies the attitudes expressed by this consensus, is itself a "veil" over the primal role of technological time in the economic process—perhaps an even deadlier one than their myth of the "veil of money" as a "neutral" commodity, rather than an independent economic motive in itself. It hardly comes as a surprise that policymakers and planners who are "hard-wired" to holding technological change as an "exogenous variable" neglect any consideration of its consequences and impact on the key economic and financial variables that *are* their conventional stock-in-trade.

This neglect by default affects two areas of policymaking more than any other. The first is employment and income stabilization; the second and worst case is the interaction of human economic behavior and its permanent consequences, *with* the natural environment and its resources. It is in this latter area that the equilibrium-field metaphor basis of neoclassical economics takes its greatest toll.

But it is precisely in terms of this vital interaction that the trade-off between "growth" and rational development takes place. They are not synonymous.

Employment and Income Stabilization Policy in the Light of the Telos-Technos Nexus

One of the earliest examples of awareness of technos' pressure on social and economic stability is that of China up to the last half of the nineteenth century. There is a great wealth of material available on the economic and technological history of Chinese civilization from both Western and Asian sources. For our purposes only a particular direction for investigation is suggested, rather than an attempt to do justice to the subject in such a brief reference.

Even the most cursory examination of the subject leads any observer to be favorably impressed by the continuous record of technical and proto-scientific innovation and ingenuity in China's culture of creativity. But parallel, absorptive development in the operational telos of Chinese economic behavior seems intermittent at best and often stationary for centuries at a stretch.

From the perspective of this exposition of the economic process, the Chinese system of social values dampened the receptivity of their consumers and institutions as effective economic carriers of their remarkable capacity for technical progress. In terms of Chapter Two, thresholds of consumption remained more or less fixed in their vital interaction with China's technological time. Category 2 of the CCSL and Sector 2 of omega remained relatively inactive in exploiting opportunities for real economic growth, but Chinese technical innovations diffused across the established routes of trade and commerce and in more receptive hands became increasingly sophisticated and practical on a vast scale via the artisan-incremental content of $\mathcal{T}$; instead of being discouraged and dampened in its feedback relationship with Telos. It can be argued that the "Chinese vector" was the obverse of J.S. Mill's advocacy of dampening technos so that the CCSL could catch up with it. The Chinese value system emphasized the maintenance of harmony and stability at any price; this factor was the hidden boundary condition of the Chinese Telos-Technos nexus. The explanations of Weber and Tawney account in large part for the more robust and *sustained* operational telos of Western societies—and there was no lack of variable response there!

The reader should recall from Chapter Four that actual levels of employment at a given point in technological time were not congruent with the boundary condition described as the Natural Participation rate. In effect, no automatic congruency is assumed about socially desirable targets for employment and what is "natural" or "warranted." And it is precisely this zone between N_r and desired employment and income levels that is the domain of rational and constructive policymaking—free of illusions about the "automaticity" of correcting forces or the "control freak" mentality of fiat government, which is just as susceptible to Veblen's warning about reactions of the "disturbed" being more disturbing than the original "disturbance" as "animal sprits" in the civil economy. This "zone" for policymaking has now become the art of walking a tightrope between the need for maintaining reasonable—not dictated or guaranteed—stability and the *moral* imperative of reducing government's power to interfere with privately made economic choices, to the bare minimum. It is hardly a new trade-off in economic history . . . just far more difficult and fraught with the risk of Veblen's warning. Hayek and Friedman must be taken very seriously on that point.

In "walking the tightrope," the point of view described herein can do no more than suggest somewhat different avenues of investigation than have been pursued under the neoclassical dispensation.

1. When the required (fixed) capital-to-output ratio is falling through Technological time, and the role of vast mega projects is consequently declining as a conservateur of employment and income levels outside the multiplier (see Chapter Three, Black Box Technologies), then the role of government would more wisely direct their policies toward cheapening the prices of goods and services in Category 2 of the CCSL . . . i.e., contribute to a lowering of the critical increment. This might take the form of being less judgmental and restrictive about the phenomenon of consumer credit and more flexible about sales taxes on commodities in Category 2. Indirectly, this would reduce the contribution of "default savings" to the total savings that consumers consciously *choose* to save from the other legitimate reasons motivating the propensity to save. Indeed, an *increased* fear of volatility could of itself reinforce the precautionary motive and, in chain reaction, the paradox of thrift phenomenon; this is a choice individuals make. Government fiat should not even give the appearance of intending to dictate or even manipulate such choosing, however altruistic it thinks its motives really are.

2. The benefits of debt accumulation by all levels of government are highly subjective, and their consequences, in terms of aggressive taxation policies, often suggest a subliminal belief that the multiplier effect of government spending will *automatically* exceed the negative multiplier effect of taxing it out of the hands of the private sector. This is a perception of negligible opportunity costs arising from the acts of government; the "track record" of history does not confirm such

perceptions. See *Public Principles of Public Debt* by James Buchanan, 1958.

3. There may be more to fear from the volatility caused by over-investment and surrogate inflation of assets than from the traditional sources of commodity inflation. Perhaps government should rely less on commodity-based and value-added taxes and more on the use of taxes derived from the proceeds of over-investment and surrogate inflation of assets. But caution and judgement are crucial. After all, such policies may increase choices for consumers—especially those associated with Category 2 of the CCSL. They *do* restrict the choices of investors . . . a fine line to walk indeed.

4. Societal norms regarding the benefits of some forms of labor as opposed to others should become more relaxed if the flow of 'Jechnological time is positive and tends to make labor *in general* a less scarce factor of production. There are a significantly large number of industries that are labor intensive by nature and whose marginal productivity is less exactly calculated than is the standard in other sectors. Many of them are heavily concentrated in the public sectors or are subsidized directly and indirectly by various levels of government in the form of tax benefits (health care, educational services, care and maintenance of existing assets and utilities, etc.). These occupations form a legitimate "employment cushion" between N_r and E; with a decent respect for the taxpayers' rights of choice, it is still possible to spare such labor the more stringent judgements of efficiency and productivity that are more appropriate to other industries, where the innovators' risk propensities and the entrepreneur's competitive edge are indispensable. A little "featherbedding" may go a long way.

5. The continuous political jostling between those who perceive extractions from the public purse as a "zero sum game" takes a new twist if examined in the perspective of the Telos-Technos nexus. For example, what is considered to be esoteric teleologies, such as Space programs, alternative energy and resource conservation projects, promotion of arts, and cultural pursuits are often condemned by critics as being in open competition with the more real needs of social pro-

grams for the poor and disadvantaged—a kind of contemporary version of the Marxian "rate of exploitation" redistributing allegedly surplus funds from the public purse to the very members of those classes who already control it. But from consideration of the material in Chapter Four, the *possible* benefits to society as a whole are open-ended; *initially*, and provided they *are* arrived at by a democratic, debated, choice of the collective, institutionally processed will, they do in the immediate future—the short run, so to speak—play an immediate role as a "cushion" between N_r and E.

But more importantly they have a capability for generating new commercially viable technologies and commodities for Category 2 of the CCSL even though they are generated from Sector 2 of omega. However difficult it may be for many to equate economic activity generated from a space program with that generated from conventional elements in Categories 1 and 2 of the CCSL, they are equivalent in terms of their role in the Telos-Technos nexus. In this light such esoteric teleologies are a case of managing (with risk) visualized "black box" technologies toward valid human goals—not necessarily economic ones at first (Categories 1 and 2 of the CCSL) in the conventional sense. But their probability of achieving some measurable benefit within a reasonable time frame (not the "long run") is far higher than repairing the negative results of some type of botched, ill-conceived "social program" or monetary tinkering, which inevitably contributes more to the environment of uncertainty and fear of the future than the "instability" they were designed to evade. In this respect, government spending from *Sector* two of omega can act as an authentic economic catalyst for Categories 1 and 2 of the CCSL. But government abuses its role in the economic process when it attempts to make the world safe from economic uncertainty by circumscribing the legitimate choices of civil society and stigmatizing the market forces that discipline it. Alternatively, those who emphasize the use of government power in the economy as the "ultimate sanction" (J.S. Mill's phrase) partake of the Socialist myth that a market economy, capitalist or otherwise, is possessed by a kind of hostile vitalism, a will of its own, which is essentially malicious, chaotic, and hostile to the interests of society— and the well-intentioned teleologies of those who would be its saviors.

Telos and Technos—A Natural "Fit" With the Economics of Development

By willfully excluding any consideration of real, event-laden, irreversible time, the neoclassical equilibrium "lock-in" has made *itself* exogenous to all rational analysis of development economics. About all their "paradigm" is capable of is to interpret all development in terms of "growth"–"no growth" in the levels of successive equilibrium states separated by dead, unexplained clock time. Consequently, most of their commentary on the subject, no matter how abstruse, reduces itself to a vague faith in technology as a "free good"—equivalent to a cargo cult rescuer from the consequences of human economic behavior through irreversible time. Perfect substitutability of commodity choices and resource endowments for the production function will always be available for insatiable, automatically compensating consumers (see Chapter Three, Appendix 16) . . . and these underlying, unspoken assumptions in themselves account for an almost blind faith that "warranted growth" in incomes will *automatically* appear to absorb any increase in the productive capacity of the economy (see Chapter Three, Appendix 4). In the light of the Telos-Technos interaction, the preceding observations are one more demonstration of the gestalt nature of the subject. After all, what possible meaning can be assigned to a process of aggregating all the successive equilibrium states through gaps of unconnected, dead clock time to a current "quantified" state? If the neoclassical "paradigm" had any real empirical value, this procedure should at least be possible, in principle. Thus, by being time-indifferent and equivalently outside technological time, neoclassical economics also rendered itself analytically indifferent to any interaction with its natural environment, including its man-made component.

Since equilibrium analysis amounts to little more than an a-temporal tautology, it cannot deal with processes that are time-path dependent, gestalt, and contingent, with respect to their end-states . . . i.e., an authentic development economics that does not make growth congruent with development and does *not* exclude the "passenger pigeon scenario."

By way of example: McCulloch's "law" tautologizes the economic history of consumption. It allows for a predictable automatic hysteresis ("period of adjustment") where the outcome after clock-time lag "t + 1" is certain. That is, the "aggregate" of "representative" consumers will automatically (in determined phase?) buy right up to the augmented productive capacity of the "production function" (not "process"). For all practical purposes, we are adding nothing to our knowledge of the real (economic) world . . . only one more baleful statement that "there is a one-to-one correspondence between clock-time and economic growth ≡ progress ≡ development.

If a "thumbnail" summation of the difference between a Telos-Technos process and the neoclassical–equilibrium "paradigm" were offered, one could probably do no better in the same space than:

Telos-Technos	Neoclassical Equilibrium/Field
Naturally Asymmetric	Forced Symmetry*
Hysteresis, Natural	Instantaneously and simultaneously determined (see Appendix 7)
Gestalt (see Appendix 4)	Aggregatable (see Appendix 8)
Technology arises from human behavior—a primal force in itself.	It's just a "residual operator" in a timeless "determined" exchange matrix
Time-Path Dependent	Absolute—Time-Path "Independent"— i.e., Real Time doesn't exist
Contingent Economic Behavior	Automatic Compensation

The "Cargo cult" rescue function played by technology in an equilibrium-field metaphor straitjacket leads *automatically* to a cavalier dismissal of any *opportunity costs* (see Appendix 4) associated with degradation of the environment because, from such a perspective they are exogenous to the "Scope and Methodology of Political Economy" just as the technology ("given" on a menu of virtual techniques without ontogeny in a timeless economic universe) that caused them is exogenous. Consequently, in the neoclassical philosophy, any given technology that optimizes production ought to be exploited to its limit, because its output

---

* The reader should compare the Keynesian constant of consumers' automatic insatiability, MPC = 1, with the notion of forced symmetry in economic thought. Is MPC = 1 an example of it ? . . . for purposes of analytic tractability?

will be consumed "in the long run," and it has no significant opportunity costs. Neoclassical economic thinking *cannot* possibly lead anywhere else without denying its underlying foundations of "insatiability" of consumers' wants and automatic compensation and re-absorption of any displaced labor caused by such optimal exploitation of a "given" technology—especially if it is associated with "growth." But is such growth rational *development*, which *must* include preservation of *natural* capital as a logical extension of a Telos-Technos explanation of the economic process—in which the "passenger pigeon scenario" is *not* exogenous to the universe of economic events and where opportunity costs *exist* as a collateral *variable* of Technological time? A potential scenario is possible in a Telos-Technos nexus, wherein a trade-off is feasible *between* a more labor-intensive technique (or technologies) that is *not* optimal in the neoclassical sense, but is *preferable* within the Telos-Technos dispensation—*and* the optimal technology in the (virtual) neoclassical sense (see Appendix 6), because opportunity costs associated with the "optimal" technical choice are real events in technological *time* and *not* exogenous to the cause and effect flow of economic history. Such a scenario is inconceivable by locking oneself in to the timeless equilibrium paradigm, just as involuntary unemployment and real business cycles are as well. Indeed, in a T/$\mathcal{T}$ nexus an optimizing choice of exploitive technology could be wealth-reducing rather than wealth-enhancing, precisely because of the illusion of "growth" as congruent with development. The reader should consult Appendix 9 for further development of such empirical case histories.

There is no better forum for this kind of analysis than the case history tradition followed by schools of business and public administration for most of the twentieth century. Although we can scarcely do justice to this subject in the few remaining pages, consider for *further investigation* the following two cases, with which virtually all readers are reasonably familiar, and for which voluminous literature exists from the specialized perspectives of the ecologist, ichthyologist and transportation planner.

1. The Case of Optimal Fishing Technologies

This is a particularly appropriate case because conflicts and demographic upheavals related to food supply are part of the legacy of Mankind since prehistoric times. Moreover, there is no better illustration of the insidious consequences of carrying over the mindset of "automaticity" and perfect "self-regulating" mechanisms from the Say/Walras equilibrium economy of mankind into a corresponding relationship between it and the economy of the "natural" world. Such an unwarranted extension of the automaticity syndrome is, of course, the analytical equivalent of making the natural environment's endowments exogenous to the workings of the man-made economy—just as technos, the Promethean imperative, is made exogenous to the perfectly self-regulating Say/Walras economy of "neo-classical" political economy.

Part of the technological legacy of the Battle of the Atlantic during World War II was the commercial development of "tracking" and surveillance techniques applicable to maximizing catches in the fisheries industries. When this was combined with the ichthyologists' knowledge of large group movements and breeding cycles of commercially valuable species—*plus* the cruder "artisan-incremental" techniques of wide-area netting and scouring the sea-beds of coastal waters—what emerged was the equivalent of what buffalo hunters armed with lever action repeating rifles did to the "numberless" herds of buffalo on the great plains of the North American Continent. If carried to its potential limits it would be equivalent to an amplification of the "passenger pigeon scenario" without parallel, and without the "cargo-cult" guarantee of rescue by a perfectly corresponding augmentation of the fish farming industries—unless we are willing to take a chance on the myths of perfect product and factor substitutability with no opportunity costs incurred by pursuing this option. But this option is a logical extension of the neoclassical legacy of unexplained factor endowments and is symmetrical with the "fundamental optimism" of "re-absorption" expressed in Appendix 4 and Chapter Three . . . any takers? After all, *it would be* "growth"—*while it lasted*, in the neoclassical sense.

2. The Case of the Automobile Industry

Another interesting case is that of the world-wide automobile industry's capability of producing tens of millions of vehicles annually and adding them to the existing fleets. In this case, the teleological drives affecting the consumption accumulation process of motor vehicles (Chapter Two, Category 2 of the CCSL) would enter into a head-on collision with environmental limitations, especially in the densely populated and crudely urbanized societies of the "third world." The industrial and sociological history of the mass markets for motor vehicles is well known in the more "developed" markets of America, Europe, and Japan. Especially in view of the ongoing debate between those who emphasize the virtues of refining the public transportation infrastructure as opposed to those who emphasize the freedom of choice and employment benefits of private transportation . . . not to mention the energy producing industries. The Gordion Knot solution to this dilemma probably lies with the fifth example given in the table of "black box" technologies in Chapter Three. But can it be assumed that there would be no significant opportunity costs associated with that option?

The preceding material does not question the neoclassical orthodoxy that growth is congruent with development; no other conclusion is derivable from the basic premises of neoclassical *political* economy, in spite of its pretensions to the "hard scientific" status of mid-nineteenth century energy physics, so thoroughly debunked by Mirowski, Wong, et al since the 1970s, and others before them as they so rigorously prove.

What is being stated unequivocally is that, in terms of the basic premises of the Telos-Technos nexus, "growth" and "development" are in one of the most vital *trade-off* relationships of the economic process: whose solutions, for good or bad, will be determined by human beings operating through their imperfect institutions and behaving as a consequence of their natural inabilities to predict the outcomes of their own complex interactions. That is, they cannot be simply "aggregated" in non-gestalt fashion, to a more or less determined end.

Consider, as a thumb-nail summary of the preceding section, Figure 6.1. *Opportunity costs* (see Appendix 5) associated with striving for the maximum growth rate offered by full exploitation of all opportunities contained by successive "era" cuts of ꝶ. The "curves" are schematic only. Obviously, a full qualitative description is not reducible to a "score" or a "graphic." The domain of Figure 6.1 is micro-economic, most appropriately by industry group (e.g., fisheries, transportation, public and private energy fuels, livestock etc.).

The role of policy in the growth vs. development trade-off is to "navigate the zone" between the growth curves and the set of opportunity–cost curves corresponding to each of them. In practice, such curves can be reasonably estimated from the economic and technological history of each industry group. Very generally, they would be quite finite in number and not unmanageably numerous and diverse. Such a schematic representation can only result from treating development and growth as trade-offs—not as absolute, mutually reinforcing, Janus-faced variables, equivalent to automatic congruency. From the perspective of Figure 6.1,

Figure 6.1

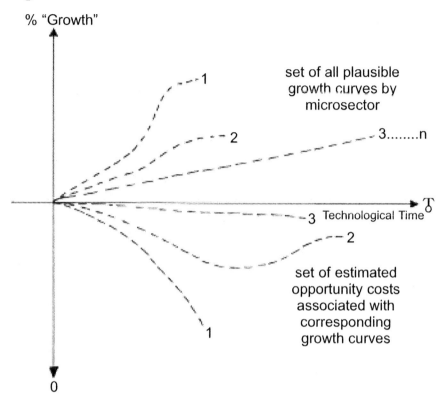

stubbornly high thresholds of consumption for particular elements offered in Category 2 of the CCSL (see Chapter Two), however irrational and Savonarola-like to the "law" of automatic compensation and its community of faith, can, under *particular* opportunity cost scenarios, constitute the better part of wisdom.

An Apocalyptic Digression—What if the "Zone" in Figure One is not Navigable?

Consider a scenario arising from any one of the following conditions or combinations thereof:

1. Inability to control population growth to satisfactory levels. When opportunity costs become penitents' costs.

2. A cataclysmic diminution in the availability of previously "taken for granted" resources, such as arable land, potable water, natural protein supply (fisheries as a non-depletable, never scarce resources).

3. Group conflict so prolonged and intense that the ultimate expression of the hegemony of the collective will is permanently imposed—decreeing *Category* 1 of the CCSL in its most frugal form—*rationing,* with Category 2 of the CCSL proscribed.

There is no assumption of virtual substitutability of productive factors, or the automatic response of technos as a "cargo-cult" rescuer from cataclysmic scarcity, as inferred from the field metaphor.

What would be expected from such an apocalyptic scenario is the equivalent to a retreat of technological time. Depending on what particular combinations of cataclysmic conditions operate, the resulting prognosis would converge to some mix of the following end states.

1. Population would be reduced to some "Malthusian" level compatible with the cataclysmic scarcity of vital resources.

2. Depending on just what resources were scarcest and their relative impacts on population reduction, the elements of Category 1 of the CCSL would be relinquished in approximately reverse order to their acquisition, through the previously positive flow of technological time. The end state would be a much reduced population surviving at the barest levels of physical subsistence. Even the cognitive content of technological time would retreat into dormancy, as the operational telos (ω) of society in all its sectors and categories provides no further causal teleologies. This degree of societal demoralization is is equivalent to a complete loss of vitality and capability of the Promethean imperative . . . in effect it is dying.

Appendix 1

Arguably, the tautologies that Keynes had built into his system were expressions of Say's law, *set up initially* as an unimpeded circular flow (a sort of straw man) from which the implicit assumptions that automatically "tautologized" it could then be siphoned away in subsequent periods as hemorrhages, e.g., $I_t < S_{t-1}$. In this way the succeeding period's income (Y_{t+1}) would be less than the income Y at (t-1) on account of a correspondingly weakened multiplier effect. The justification for the leakage that begat the diminished income was essentially a buttressing of Malthus's fears regarding the propensity to save more than was justified *by the classes who could afford to save.* In Keynes' version the classical symmetry between savings and income was shattered by imposing a different functional relationship on the propensity to invest the money described as savings; i.e., investment became a function of prevailing and "expected" returns: not just the same constant percentage of income, as was savings; nor in a similar functional relationship with prevailing rates of return, as savings was presumed to be under the classical dispensation. With the Walrasian boundary conditions firmly locked in (constancy of technology and tastes) as Keynes stated at the beginning of Chapter 18 of *The General Theory*, 1936, where else could he have turned to explain how business cycle crises dragged the economy down from initial positions of "full employment equilibrium"? Indeed, Keynes' efforts to intensify the "blame" on investors' uncertainty of expectations led to much discussion of whether Keynes was a "closet" radical subjectivist refusing to disclose himself to his contemporary "Austrian" colleagues. See *The Philosophy of Keynes' Economics*, Routledge, 2003, ISBN 0-415-28153-9 and 415-31244-2. Also consult Jochen Runde on the same subject. Refer back to Ludwig Lachmann and Adolph Lowe on the same dilemma at the end of Chapter Five.

Appendix 2

In this respect, Mill was exercising his prerogative, in the British tradition, of allowing "moral" imperatives a wider berth than the rigidly logical. The reader should refer back to the similar circumstances regarding Keynes mentioned earlier in this chapter; like Mill, Keynes was no acolyte when it came to the rigors of formal logic, mathematical or otherwise.

Appendix 3

Roy Harrod's concepts of "Warranted growth rates" of income and "Natural" rates of growth are especially interesting in the context of the Telos-Technos process. Indeed a critical re-evaluation of his concepts is "warranted" in terms of the material in Chapter Four, especially Figures 4.3 to 4.6. Although one cannot do justice to the subject in the brief space of an appendix, several comments are in order. Harrod, in a classic example of Hume's guillotine, identifies the "natural" rate of income growth with that generated by full employment of all available factors of production at the *macro-economic level*. But he introduces "autonomous" investment into a model whose initial boundary condition appears to have been in our terms, $\mathcal{T}$ held constant. But autonomous investment is a vehicle of technological improvement, in addition to the increase in productive capacity attributable to induced (and presumably constant vintage) *capital* investment. Thus "warranted" growth rates in income appear to be what is required to *absorb* (via the law of automatic compensation?) the product of increased capacity, so as to maintain something close to full employment, another initial boundary condition in his model. Arguably, Harrod was groping for an explanation of secular stagnation within the framework of boundary conditions that could not possibly lead to it. Perhaps he was, in twentieth century terms, engaged in a replay of Ricardo's and Mill's doubts regarding the law of "automatic compensation" as the logical rejoinder to the "machinery" question. In that sense he was on the right track.

Appendix 4

The gestalt nature of economic life always goes together with "purposive" (Menger et al) goal- and image-directed (Whitehead and Samuel Alexander & Bergson) human action, however humble and short-lived or grandiose in "vision" the resultant transactions and exchanges are. This is why *all* intervention by the state is not necessarily a gross "intrusion" into the "free" domain of economic life—if the "goals" of the "collectivity" require the tools and knowledge of economic "agents" . . . this is really what "Sector 2" of omega is all about (see Chapter Two). Such "intrusions" are often "conservative" in nature, such as the "keeping the lid on function" in times of economic and social instability (a heavyweight consideration for Keynes and Weiser who quite rightly feared for the fragile nature of civilized restraint) or in conflicts with other societies and nations . . . simply part of the human condition. Or as Veblen might have put it: "We cannot 'isolate' the 'economic interest' from 'the organic whole' of all 'other interests.'" In effect, societal goals and needs cannot be "arithmomorphically" (Georgescu-Roegen's term) aggregated from the consequences of individual (micro) goals and needs. Even the market . . . probably the second oldest of all human institutions, just as Phoroneus understood, has its limitations. And much of the need for a "keeping-the-lid-on function" would never exist if the self-correcting-underlying and "built-in" gyroscope of the extreme libertarians was an empirical reality, instead of an "ideal" built into the Say/Walras benchmark paradigm. Put another way, this kind of "mechanistic" perspective on economic life can easily stagger into Henri Bergson's definition of the "comical—the encrustation of the mechanical on the living." Connoisseurs of "lost causes, last stands and bitter ends" should be reminded that even the "market" has a frightening potential for irreversible chaos and that M. Bergson began his intellectual career as a deterministically inclined mathematical prodigy. He wasn't the only one.

Appendix 5

Fredrich Von Wleser's [2] Powerful Idea and Its "Good Fit" with the Telos-Technos Nexus*

Because of its capability for useful projection into unexplored areas of economic application (provided "real" event-laden time is acknowledged as the only basis of a truly dynamic economic "paradigm"), an extension of the opportunity cost idea has been used to advantage in a Telos-Technos explanation of how the "world" works . . . i.e., a non-tautological explanation of the interaction of the man-made economy with the "natural" environment, which both neoclassical economics—with its flight-from-real-time "mental block" and the not unrelated Marxist syndrome—could not even begin to address in a coherent inclusive manner. (He considered that capitalist technical advance would automatically would solve despoilation and resource exhaustion problems. Heard this more recently?) We may recall that the opportunity cost idea was employed by Menger's twentieth century successors to great advantage in shooting down the "opposition" during the "socialist-calculation debate"—even in its primordial form, i.e., the need of the planner/investor to compare a choice of "plan" with what benefits are foregone by not choosing a competing alternative. This is the inherently "immovable" barrier for even the most determined "well-intentioned" cock-sure legion of fiat style planners. There are no benchmarks of any kind to compare the consequences of one set of actions with another in the "events-are-the-time" real world (e.g., prices, quantities, and differences in kind of commodities, different goals, etc.) In short, all the myriad variables that Menger emphasized are the stuff of legitimate complexity that "makes the (economic) world go (not necessarily) round" . . . and necessitated Phoroneus's "invention" of the marketplace . . . the eldest "daughter" of "spontaneous order.

---

*   It should be recalled that Von Wieser was the least inclined of all the "Austrian-School" economists to the "libertarian" Renaissance of "laissez-faire" economic policies. He had a well known fear of the fragility of social stability and the roots of destabilization. Recall that Keynes feared that no society could stand up to more than five years of high unemployment levels.

The concept of opportunity costs is an ideal carrier for at least one of the ways by which the "entropy" principle (the tendency in all systems toward "running downhill" into disorder, instability, chaos, etc.) expresses itself *as* economic events, without staggering into the gross and fatal error of trying to describe its presence in economic life in terms of a physics metaphor. *Economic concepts can and should be used to explain economic events* (the principle of "sui generis"—George Shackle). The instability engendered by episodes of mass involuntary unemployment, explained in Chapter Four, has other deeply rooted, dynamic, path-dependent "structural" roots that cannot be directly related to Wieser's powerful idea . . . and for which a "keeping-the-lid-on" strategy must be worked out, without the Polyanna fantasy of believing in the great automatic gyroscope "in-the-sky:" the Austrian school's analogue to the new-classical belief in technology as a "free good"—a *de facto* "cargo-cult" rescuer from "the tragedy of the commons," or the "passenger pigeon scenario." Underlying this other expression of the "entropy principle" in the trajectory of economic history is another basic idea about human behavior: namely that, to a greater or lesser extent, in all human beings and their "all-too-human" collectivities and institutions, there exists a certain reservoir of exploitable "Promethean" energy . . . perhaps "adding-up" to something more than the "sum of its individual parts" when driven by the "right" goals/teleologies: And that these innate Promethean drives need outlets or at the very least some kind of legitimately sanctioned "lid" on them—especially if they are frustrated to any significant degree by forces beyond their "short-run" control. If neither of these two "solutions" is forthcoming (as in "quick-fix") then society may have to cope with a "Pandora's box" scenario . . . not exactly a stranger to the history of civilization. This seems deeply held by the Japanese.

We well ask why even the most impressive luminaries of the Austrian School overlooked this powerful insight by "one of their own" and didn't apply it to the interaction of the economy of humankind with that of "Mother Nature." As well as pressing forward with Schumpeter's pristine undeveloped ideas about technological development, by rescuing them from the quicksand of pseudo-reconciliation with the Walrasian general equilibrium/field "paradigm"??

For convenience's sake we can subdivide the extensions of the "opportunity cost" idea into three classes.

1. *Consumers' Opportunity Cost.* e.g., *Foregoing* the pleasure of eating a dozen jelly beans because the consumer prefers a small chocolate truffle. Economics 101.
2. *Environmental Opportunity Cost.* This is the one most closely related to choice of productive technology and discloses itself as resource exhaustion (tragedy of the commons, the passenger pigeon scenario) or serious collateral spoilation of the natural and human (urban and rural) environments.
3. *Social* opportunity costs, or the art of "keeping the lid on" arising from the consequences of societal choices, producers, consumers, or government, especially as they impact the natural employment rate and public health (physical and "psychic"—John Maynard Keyne's favorite usage.)

Arguably, the introduction of any economic change whatsoever (Technos or Telos) generates uncertainty, regardless of the degree to which such uncertainty can be reduced to "risk" (i.e., the calculus of probability)* above and beyond that which previously existed; "opportunity costs" have been generated. This was probably what upset the gods of Olympus and "did-in" Prometheus—and undermined the "Chinese Vector."

Link the material from Chapter Three, Figure 3.5 with the idea of opportunity costs in Chapter Six . . . to produce a situation where choices of technology are made and executed not because of the "one-upsmanship" required in a desperate conflict situation, but as a "rational" choice to avoid highly destructive opportunity costs. This concordance may be further developed into a "rationale" for "unchoosing" particular "high efficiency" technologies in terms of direct one-dimensional "t" costs and replacing them with more "labor-intensive" technologies that are indisputably justified because of their capability to be less disruptive and negative in terms of opportunity costs.

It is important that these scenarios be lined with historical examples of (both analysis and deliberate "harmonious" choice) social and ethical policies. From the text-manuscript these are:

---

* In approximate concordance with Frank Knight's distinction between the two related—but hardly identical—concepts.

1. John Stewart Mill's suggested policy of slowing down the introduction of labor-saving "machinery." That is, Mill was literally "too smart in spite of himself" to swallow- hole the super-"ergodic" assumptions underlying McCulloch's "law" of automatic compensation . . . i.e., one "law" too many, even for economics.

2. The "Chinese-vector" (cultural choices made transcendant policy) discussed in Chapter Six . . . an interesting historical example indeed, of fear of the "Promethean imperative" and a remarkable analogue of what the gods of Olympus did to poor old Prometheus for, in effect, challenging their "authority."

Appendix 6

The reader should apply the schematic representations shown in Chapter Four, Figures 4.3 to 4.6 to this trade-off scenario. It is possible to create a "policy solution" to particularly imminent and threatening environmental problems while side-stepping the more intrusive taxation strategies. In such a scenario, employment would probably increase—inadvertently, not in the "feather-bedding" sense of the Jananese "solutions" (see *Dogs and Demons, Tales from the Dark Side of Japan*, by Alex Kerr and Karen Van Wolferen. 2001, Hill and Wang). But aggregate income as measured by conventional national accounting procedures would propbably remain the same—or even decrease. See Chapter Four and Samuel Hollander's discussion of John Stuart Mill's recognition of the problem.

Hint: Combine these schematic figures with the material about unacceptable "opportunity costs" arising from exploiting productive technologies "ad extremum." Is it feasible to illustrate the consequences of such policy solutions in terms of counter-clockwise arcs swung back (i.e., upwards) from an initial (developmentally superceded?) historical position? Voilà! Positive development, in terms of checking environmental despoilation, without "growth" in the national accounts sense of the Term? The contribution to E would result from an underlying contribution to the Natural participation rate $\rightarrow N_r$ . . . keeping in mind that employment is a societally chosen distribution of benefits from the N_r.

Appendix 7

Hysteresis and Its Relationship to the (Economics? of) the "Assymetric-Informaton" Syndrome "Paradigm Shift"?

The Telos-Technos nexus is not compatible with the assymetric informa-tion" syndrome. Hysteresis is a natural ingredient of the *human condi-tion*. Transaction costs are, in effect, some of the normal costs of hyster-esis; so are the costs of "shopping." So are the various forms of insurance, warranties, and every institution that tries to dampen the uncertainty that arises from economic actions of any kind. The classical economists called periods of hysteresis "periods of adjustment," although they tended to exaggerate their predictability and the automaticity of the outcome. There-fore, "assymetric information" is not an unnatural barrier to the Say/Walras "debouchement" whose "smoothing-out" would in effect restore the neoclassical "standard model" (physics mimicry again?) to its nor-mal gyroscopic self. Hayek was dead-on when he identified assymetric *knowledge* as the stuff of "discovery" in the market; what tacit knowl-edge, a good working price system, spontaneous order, etc. brings to-gether with surprisingly little direction from "omniscient" controllers. "Assymetrical knowledge" is not a target for tinkering or "remedy" by those who are attempting one more futile "game" of fossilizing the natu-ral action of real event-laden time, so that it fits neatly alongside the timeless neoclassical, static equilibrium fantasy.

It is no longer a mystery why the "Economics of Information para-digm-shifters" minimize all references to Hayek and Menger of the Aus-trian school as well as to the common sense of George Stigler on the subject.

The Austrian economists understood clearly that pooled assymetric knowledge is the "reason why" behind the natural division of labor, which is itself the stuff of spontaneous ordering when human action is set into motion by the right causal teleologies. What a convoluted "Ptolomeic" way of avoiding the issue of real-event time and the naturalness of hys-teresis! Transaction costs (or ancillary factor costs) are just part of the natural chain of economic events. They create markets themselves for various services and the kinds of labor associated with them. They don't inhibit the formation of markets. Social distrust masquerading as culture, mistaken ideologies, and the policies they lead to, do that. The history of the 20th century bears bloody witness to that.

Appendix 8

At the pinnacle of the Positivist (or is it pseudo-scientific?) metaphor in neoclassical economics, the most "advanced" practitioners became so "cocksure" of the unassailability of their fortress that they proclaimed:

a. "Once the model is simulated, a more rigorous test for the validity of the model can be made . . . by comparing *the time series* generated by the model against the actual observed behavior of the system." Or:
b. "Once the reduction of the system to its individual decision-making 'units' (do the authors mean human beings? has been accomplished, there is a great hope for a solution of the aggregation problem. Thus through computer models we see the possibility of developing working models of the economy that will have a solid empirical basis."
c. ". . . we are generally not interested in tracing through the process by which equilibrium is reached, but only in deriving the equilibrium values. These values are easy to find by simple mathematical analysis."

The readers are advised to return to Chapter 3 for Norbert Wiener's wisdom on the subject.

From "Computer Models in Dynamic Economics," *Quarterly Journal of Economics*. K.J. Cohen and Richard M. Cyert, Feb. 1961. As a concordance, the reader should compare these proclamations to "The Cult Shocks as Proxies for the Exogenous . . ." Chapter Two, herein.

Appendix 9

There are other scenarios where where wealth-enhancing preservation of natural capital endowments, reduction of environmental opportunity costs and, inadvertently, more labor-intensive technologies may happily converge, as contributors to a fully justifiable higher Natural participation rate. The reader should not assume that the author is being "tongue-in-cheek."

1. A return to more intensive usage of handkerchiefs instead of the indiscriminate use of the pulp and paper-originating soft facial tissues. The chain of potential benefit in avoiding unnecessary opportunity costs is left to the reader's imagination. But its controversial aspects are predictable.
2. Proscribing the use of disposable diapers because they have generated the most notorious and obvious opportunity costs! This could occasion a return to the more labor-intensive old-time diaper services. In effect, we would be adding the equivalent of more stages of production, instead of reducing them (see Chapter Three). This too would set off a chain of acrimony similar to (1).
3. Encouraging the massive production and piped distribution (oil-pipline mode) of desalinated sea water into inland regions—even the ones which are well-acquifered—in order to preserve existing levels of water tables and lessen the pressure on existing fresh water bodies. Is this the eqivalent of a return to Roman aqueducts . . . updated? . . . to stave off The Apocalypse?
4. Encouraging the reduction of meat consumption on traditional CCSL mappings (See Chapter Two) as well as discouraging the usage of a wide variety of chemical products which are indispensable factors of production in agri-business. The combined effect of these measures would be to lessen the seepage of livestock by-products and animal wastes into ground water tables and the pristine preservation of fresh water courses and wetlands. But at what price in acrimony?
5. Promoting the use of indisputably more expensive synthetic (e.g., Pergo) building materials instead of relying on natural wood products. The chain of reduction in environmental op-

portunity costs would not necessarily be calculable in "pecuniary" terms. And the direct costs would undoubtedly have to be "absorbed" by consumers—"imputed" back to them in the fashion of Friedrich Von Wieser. But it may well be that the net contribution to the Natural participation rate from such an unconventional reversal of the productivity process— i.e., adding more stages of production into the building trades instead of reducing them—could also be beneficial to "keeping-the-lid-on" socially . . . something that Wieser would have greatly appreciated. But what would be the counter-effects of such heavy-handed policies, in terms of affecting the commodity composition of consumer demand? Would it decrease the demand for lower density housing "downstream" of the chain of economic events because we chose policies that appeared to burden consumers "upstream"?

Bibliography

Chapter One

1. Thorstein Veblen. *The Theory of the Leisure Class.*
2. John Ramsey McCulloch. *Discourse on the Rise, Progress, Peculiar Objects and Importance of Political Economy*, 1824; *On the Works of David Ricardo*, 1846; and *The Literature of Political Economy*, 1845.
3. Nicholas Georgescu Roegen. *The Entropy Law and the Economic Process*, 1976 edition.
4. Samuelson, Dorfman and Solow. *Linear Programming and Economic Analysis*, 1958.

Chapter Two

1. John Maynard Keynes. *The General Theory of Employment, Interest and Money*, 1936.
2. Roy F. Harrod. *Towards a Dynamic Economics*, 1948, MacMillan, Lecture three. The reader should note the author's version of "dynamic" at that time; i.e., it's Walrasian, little changed by the reigning paradigm since then.
3. E.D. Domar. *Capital Expansion, Rate of Growth and Employment*; Econometrica-14, 137-147: 1946.
4. John R. Hicks. *A Contribution to the Theory of the Trade Cycle*, Oxford, 1950, Chapter VI and appendix.
5. George Stigler. "Notes on the History of the Giffen Paradox." *Journal of Political Economy*, 1947. Dr. Stigler, some decades later, also contributed an appropriately belittling "note" to the history of the Assymetrical Information "paradigm-shift" by way of dismissing it as just another version of transaction costs. Compare to Appendix Seven of Chapter Six, herein.

6. John Stuart Mill. *Principles of Political Economy*, Chapter six, sections one and two.
7. Charles Babbage. *Economy of Machinery and Manufactures*, 1835.
8. David Ricardo. *Principles of Political Economy and Taxation*, Chapter 31 on "Machinery."
9. John Ramsay McCulloch. *Essay on Wages*, 1826.
10. Thorstein Veblen. *Imperial Germany and the Industrial Revolution*, 1915.
11. Joan Robinson. *Canadian Journal of Economics*, May, 1970. A classic of its kind and possibly the definitive proclamation of victory in the "Cambridge Capital Controversy."
12. Joseph Alois Schumpeter. *The Theory of Economic Development*, 1961 edition of 1911 first edition. It was a tragedy for Economics that the great, if eccentric bon-vivant Schumpeter, staggered into the quicksand of bogus-synthesis with the Walrasian neo-"classical" (?) general-equilibrium field paradigm.
13. Samuel Butler. *Erewhon*—any edition. The reader should compare Butler's solution to the unsettling consequences of technological change and consumers' tastes to J.S. Mill's initial solutions—not to mention what the Greek gods did to Prometheus, and the "Chinese Vector" . . . see Chapter Six and its accompanying bibliography from Joseph Needham on the same subject.
14. Alfred Marshall. *Principles of Ecnomics*, Chapter 2, Book 3, Chapter 3.
15. Karen I. Vaughn. *Austrian Economics in America, Migration of a Tradition*, Cambridge University Press, 1994 and 1998. The reader should enjoy her excellent treatment of Karl Menger's seminal grasp of complexity in economics. Dr. Vaughn's is hard to beat for lucidity and seamless connection to later thinkers on the same subject from the Austrian School, such as the great Friedrich Von Hayek, et al. See the next item for clarification.
16. Bruce Caldwell. *Hayek's Challenge*, University of Chicago Press, 2004.
17. Ross Ashby. *An Introduction to Cybernetics*, 1965 edition. University Paperbacks, Meththuen and Company Ltd. See Chapter Seven on "Quantity of Variety." Obviously this version cannot be applied directly to the contents of Chapter Two, herein. But it's a good starting point for an ambitious aspirant. It also provides an opportunity to

link the Menger-Hayek-Polanyi views of complexity to those of Henri Bergson and Samuel Alexander on "multiplicity;" actualization of the "virtual" into heterogeneity; emergences and novelty and their intimate connection to the dynamics of gestaltness in Economics.

Chapter Three

1. Robert Graves. *The Greek Myths*, George Braziller Inc. New York. 1959.
2. Tibor Scitovsky. *The Joyless Economy*, 1976.
3. Norbert Wiener. *The Human Use of Human Beings*, 1954 and *God and Golem*, 1964.
4. Friedrich V. Hayek. *The Sensory Order* and *Economics and Knowledge*, 1941.
5. Samuel Alexander. *Space, Time and Diety*, The Gifford Lectures, 1916-1918.
6. Dennis Gabor. *Inventing the Future*, 1963. Gabor quotes Norbert Wiener's warnings about the "almost unlimited productivity of the automated factory"—Gabor's own theories about the prospects for full employment should be compared with the current structure of the labor force, especially with the concept of the Natural Participation Rate in Chapter Four and William Vickrey's prognostications on the same subject described in the bibliography. Does Gabor's concept of things "holographic" not bear a certain relationship to things "gestalt"?
7. Karl Heinrich Marx. *Das Kapital*; I, 1: 4.
8. Henri Bergson. For a good, perhaps classic contemporary survey of his basic ideas the reader should study closely *Bergsonism*, 1988, by Gilles Deleuze. Zone Books, and MIT Press distributors.
9. The wisdom of Ludwig V. Mises will easily outlive the notorious and shabby criticisms of John Kenneth Galbraith (1949) and Paul Samuelson (1964). "Must reads" by Edler - Mises are listed below:
10. *Epistemological Problems of Economics*, 1930-34.
11. "Human Action," 1945-49, *A Treatise on Economics*.
12. *The Great German Inflation*, 1932, See review by F.D. Graham in *Economica*.
13. *The Non-Neutrality of Money*, 1938, published in English in 1982.
14. *The Treatment of Irrationality in the Social Sciences*, 1944, Philosophy of Phenomenological Research.

Chapter Four

1. Homer. *The Odyssey*, any edition, any good translation regardless of language.
2. Samuel Hollander. *The Classical Economists*, Several editions. The reader should study closely Hollander's grasp of the incomparable John Stuart Mill.
3. Jacques Barzun. *Science, The Glorious Entertainment*.
4. Mark Blaug. *Economic Theory in Retrospect* . . . especially for his lucid criticism and understanding of how the classical economists, Jean Baptiste Say, McCulloch, David Ricardo, and J.S. Mill, tried to grapple with the reality of technological employment and its impact on the welfare of working people . . . instead of staggering into conspiracy theories like Marx, or simply denying it as "exogeneous" or perhaps outside the neo-classical box.
5. William Vickrey had an ominous "feeling in his gut" about the improbability of the "full-employment" chimera, e.g., "There is no automatic equilibrium at reasonably full employment". . . *Challenge*, Vol. 36, 1993 and "Larger deficits are necessary and proper means to mitigate unemployment as the far greater evil in terms of human welfare". . . See *Industrial and Labour Relations Review*, January, 2002.

Chapter Five

1. Friedrich Von Hayek. *The Pure Theory of Capital*, 1941.
2. Piero Sraffa. *Producing Commodities by Means of Commodities*, circa 1960. This a minimal reading of Sraffa. Sraffa is universally acknowledged as having triggered the "Cambridge Capital Controversy" with all of its baleful and embarrassing consequences for the neo-classical hard-core positivists.
3. Stanislaw Andreski. *Social Sciences as Sorcery*, 1972, Andre Deutsch, The Trinity Press. . . especially Chapters 10 and 13.
4. Thorstein Veblen on the distinction between the "pecuniary" valuation of capital and its industrial utilization as capital factors of production . . . Not Veblen's terminology, but what he really meant. *Quarterly Journal of Economics* and the *Journal of Political Economy*, 1898 to 1909; Veblen at his most incisive!

Chapter Six

1. John Maynard Keynes (fils). The Galton Lectures, 1937.
2. John Nivelle Keynes (pere). *The Scope and Methodology of Political Economy*.
3. Sigfried Giedon. *Mechanization Takes Command*, 1941.
4. Joseph Needham. "Time and Knowledge in China and the West." An essay in *The Voices of Time*, 1966, George Braziller publisher. Edited by J.T. Fraser. Needham is perhaps the most famous writer on this vast and intriguing subject. But many other superb researchers have succeeded him . . . including those who have built working models of early Chinese technology. The reader should notice how explicitly Needham links technological events with the flow of time and attempts to reverse it in his text.
5. James Buchanan. *Public Principles of Public Debt*, 1958.
6. Frank Knight. *Risk, Uncertainty and Profit*, 1921: A classic of its genre . . . the reach for clarity in economic thought.
7. Michael Polanyi. *The Tacit Dimension*, 1967. Based on the 1962 Terry Lectures at Yale, 1962.

About the Author

Norman L. Roth is a native of Toronto, Ontario Canada. He is a graduate of Queen's University Kingston, Ontario (1962). He took additional graduate courses in Operations Research (1964-65) McGill University, and the University of Toronto, in Systems Analysis and Linear Programming (1967-68). His career in two levels of government, Federal and municipal includes: (1) The Dominion Bureau of Statistics, (currently Statistics Canada) as an economist in National Accounts and Balance of Payments division, and (2) The City of Toronto Planning Board as an economist-urban planner for ten years. He has also worked as a market research economist for a now-defunct but, at that time, nationwide department store chain. He was a businessman for many years in the real estate development industry and has had an ongoing career in the transportation technology industry, which led to commercially significant U.S. patents in "all-weather" control systems (independent of fixed utility hook-ups) for Diesel power plants. This in turn led to some very instructive and ongoing conflicts with several levels of government and certain transportation industries in Canada. All of this unique experience is reflected in the pages of *Telos and Technos*.